The Vietnam War

The Vietnam War

A Study in the Making of American Policy

MICHAEL P. SULLIVAN

THE UNIVERSITY PRESS OF KENTUCKY

Figure 20 is reprinted from Kjell Goldmann, "East-West Tension in Europe, 1946–1970: A Conceptual Analysis and a Quantitative Description," *World Politics* 26 (October 1973). Copyright © 1973 by Princeton University Press. Diagram 2, p. 118, reprinted with permission of Princeton University Press.

Copyright © 1985 by The University Press of Kentucky

Scholarly publisher for the Commonwealth, serving Bellarmine College, Berea College, Centre College of Kentucky, Eastern Kentucky University, The Filson Club, Georgetown College, Kentucky Historical Society, Kentucky State University, Morehead State University, Murray State University, Northern Kentucky University, Transylvania University, University of Kentucky, University of Louisville, and Western Kentucky University.

Editorial and Sales Offices: Lexington, Kentucky 40506-0024

Library of Congress Cataloging-in-Publication Data
Sullivan, Michael P.
    The Vietnam war.

    Bibliography: p.
    Includes index.
    1. Vietnamese Conflict, 1961–1975—United States.
2. United States—Foreign relations—1945–
I. Title.
DS558.S85   1985   959.704′3   85-7497
ISBN 978-0-8131-5502-9

Contents

Acknowledgments   ix

1 Vietnam: Competing Perspectives   1

2 Vietnam as Vital: Myth or Reality?   12

3 Decision-Making Models:
   Rational Policy or Quagmire?   51

4 Moods and Public Opinion:
   Background for Decisions   87

5 The Vietnam War, the Cold War,
   and Long-Term Trends   122

6 The Lessons of Vietnam   151

References   187

Index   194

Figures and Tables

FIGURES
1. Pages of Official Documents and Number of Justifications of War in the Pentagon Papers   21
2. Pages of Official Documents in *New York Times* and Gravel Editions of Pentagon Papers, 1964   23
3. Quarterly Average of Presidential Rhetoric in Documents on Vietnam   37
4. Trends in Country Reference and U.S. Casualties, 1964–1971   41
5. Perceived Scope of the Vietnam War as Reflected in Presidential Documents, 1961–1972   42
6. Quarterly Level of U.S. Casualties and Symbolic Rhetoric in Presidential Documents, 1961–1972   44
7. Quarterly Trend in Johnson's Symbolic Rhetoric and U.S. Casualties   46
8. Percentage of the State of the Union Address Devoted to Foreign Affairs, 1790–1950   92
9. Percentage of the State of the Union Address Devoted to Foreign Affairs, 1950–1984   100
10. Congressional Support for Presidential Foreign Policy, 1953–1983   104
11. Foreign Policy Bills as a Percentage of the President's Program and Rate of Success for Foreign Policy Bills, 1954–1974   106
12. Witnesses Advocating Defense Cuts, Senate Armed Services Committee and Subcommittees on Defense Appropriations, 1961–1974   108

13. Pages of Testimony Advocating Defense Cuts, Senate Armed Services Committee and Subcommittees on Defense Appropriations, 1961–1974   109
14. Responses to the Question, "Was Sending American Troops to Vietnam a Mistake?" 1966–1974   110
15. Respondents Supporting Various "Withdrawal" or "Escalation" Options, 1964–1972   112
16. Trends in Support for the War in Vietnam, by Age Group, 1965–1971   115
17. Internationalist and Isolationist Opinion, 1964–1976   120
18. Intensity of Conflict and Cooperation Behavior, United States-USSR, 1948–1973   127
19. United States-USSR Relations, 1948–1978   128
20. Goldmann's Coefficient of Imbalance for East-West Tension in Europe   133
21. Annual Amount of International War Underway, 1816–1980   140
22. Log Transformations of Battle Deaths in International and Interstate Wars Begun per Five-Year Period, 1816–1980   142
23. Symbolic Rhetoric in State of the Union Addresses, 1950–1980   161
24. Respondents Choosing Foreign Affairs as Most Important Problem, 1968–1981   168
25. Trends in Opinion about Defense Spending, 1960–1983   170
26. Annual Nation-Months of War Underway, 1816–1980   178

TABLES
1. References to Vietnam and to Other Countries in *Papers of the President*, 1946–1970   17
2. Pages on Vietnam and on Other Countries in *Britannica Book of the Year*, 1946–1970   18
3. Introvert and Extrovert Phases in U.S. Foreign Policy   91
4. Foreign Affairs as a Percentage of State of the Union Address, Introvert and Extrovert Phases   101

Acknowledgments

Thought processes, fortunately, do not occur in a vacuum, and certainly one of the fringe benefits of scholarly activity is intellectual interaction with others. This work has greatly benefited from just such interaction. Gail Bernstein, Lady Branham, and Ole Holsti read the entire manuscript and provided very useful suggestions. Numerous discussions with Randolph Siverson helped in many ways. Susan Diffenderfer's professional skill as a graphic artist shows up in all of the illustrations that follow. Mary Sue McQuown not only typed the manuscript and therefore kept it on track in a purely mechanical way, she also made sure that what I really wanted to say got said. Finally, as with so much of the work that came out of the University of Arizona's Political Science department from 1979 to 1984, Susan Johnston was truly the unsung heroine.

I am grateful to all of these people. Any errors that may have crept in are, of course, my own responsibility.

To the memory of

Raymond W. Sullivan (1950–1969)
 Sp. 4. United States Army

And to the many other
casualties of the Vietnam War

1. Vietnam: Competing Perspectives

On 30 April 1975, as American diplomats and Marines were being hastily lifted off the roof of the American embassy in Saigon into helicopters under heavy enemy fire, an era in American foreign policy was ignominiously coming to an end. The United States was exiting South Vietnam in the most undignified manner possible—short of military defeat in 1973. And yet, almost immediately, as someone later remarked, Americans turned off the Vietnam War as easily as they turn off their television sets. A curious feeling of noncaring followed the war.

In the winter of 1982, *Washington Post* columnist Philip Geyelin commented on a CBS documentary entitled "The Uncounted Enemy: A Vietnam Deception," in which it was alleged that there had been a high-level plan within the military and intelligence establishments to "knowingly and systematically understate enemy force levels. The idea was to preserve the impression back home that the war was being won." And so, Geyelin remarked, subordinates resorted to "falsification of facts" and "rigging" intelligence estimates; estimates of enemy strength were "negotiated" between rival bureaucracies "for the sake of appearances."

Geyelin then raised several questions concerning the techniques used by CBS in putting together the documentary, and noted that the dispute between the network and those interviewed in the program degenerated into a dispute over technicalities, and then the whole issue between network and former government officials suddenly sank from sight. He quoted former U.S. ambassador to Saigon Ellsworth Bunker, who said it was "just like the old days," one more clash between the press and the government.

And that, Geyelin noted, is the point. Whereas the network had set out to show that there had in fact been a conscious conspiracy at the highest levels of government to suppress and mislead, and that it had been successful, "the net effect was to demonstrate, yet one more time, that apart from a relative handful of those directly involved, nobody much cares." Geyelin paraphrased in his column one of the original motivations for undertaking the present work: it has become evident that, for whatever reasons, "almost nobody—not yesterday's leaders nor today's and still less the American public—is yet ready to confront the 'only war we ever lost' in a civil and instructive search for the reasons why" (*Sacramento Bee*, 18).

Until recently, this neglect of what was the major event in American foreign policy of the past generation has been very disquieting, although understandable given the trauma and the devastation of the war. It became one of the lengthiest foreign involvements of this nature for the United States in its history, resulting in over 56,000 American deaths, untold hundreds of thousands of other deaths, and many more wounded. It wracked a nation for a half dozen years; and even into the early 1980s, the "Vietnam vet" syndrome was still causing grief and agony for many of those who had been involved in the war, as well as for their families and friends.

In other words, the war was a costly failure. It achieved few of the stated goals set out by American foreign policy decision makers. Certainly one could not argue that no goals were achieved. Perhaps simply the presence of such a large United States force accomplished certain goals, such as the defeat of the Communist party in 1965 in Indonesia, although one cannot say for sure. Certainly such goals were uppermost in decision makers' minds. But nonetheless, the primary outcome that those decision makers were attempting to prevent—at least if we believe their rhetoric on the war—did come about, namely the domination by one or more Communist nations of much of Southeast Asia. And yet, until very recently, there has been little serious, sustained, and broad-ranging analysis of this failure (Ravenal 1978).

Even in mid-1980, an Associated Press story indicated that a thirteen-part history of the war planned by WGBH-TV of *Boston* might have to be shortened because "neither business nor government wants to bankroll the project" (*Arizona Daily Wildcat* 29 July 1980, 15). The program manager for WGBH-TV said, "I think Vietnam sends shudders through the frame of corporate America. I guess companies are afraid it may open wounds."

The project was ultimately funded and broadcast in the fall of 1983. Several other programs, as well as articles and books analyzing the war, appeared at that time. Still Vietnam constituted a major American foreign involvement stretching over almost a generation, which—with the recent exceptions—seemed to have faded from public memory.

In addition to this apparent public indifference, many of the analyses that have cropped up almost a decade after the war (including the WGBH-TV series) have focused on certain types of questions and approaches. Why did the United States "lose" in Vietnam? What were the so-called turning points that dragged the United States into the war? Did the United States fail to "try hard enough"? Was Lyndon Johnson the one who brought about the war? Other questions focused on the "roots" of the conflict, and whether, in some predetermined way, they could be traced all the way back to decisions made in the late 1940s. Did domestic issues take precedence? Were the Vietcong truly independent, or, as maintained by the administration at the time, tools of the North Vietnamese? Answers to each of these questions might prove interesting in understanding a relatively narrow field of inquiry concerning the American involvement in Vietnam, but by and large they aid little in addressing some more broadly-conceived questions.

Although more specific research questions may have been the original driving force behind some of the evidence produced for this book, the greatest motivation was a feeling that Vietnam had not been confronted in a forthright way, that too many narrow questions had been asked about the American involvement there, and that for too many years it had been turned off like a television set. To ignore the war, however, or to ask only simple or narrow questions about it—itself has implications for how the public and American leaders view United States foreign policy.

Not only the war but also the war's veterans were being relegated to obscurity, which is yet another indicator of how Americans seemed to be dealing with the war. Veterans' benefits were for years under assault in the United States Congress. The bitterness of some veterans against the system that sent them off to fight manifested itself in January 1981 when Americans who had been held hostage in the Iranian embassy in Tehran were released. Many veterans seethed when they saw "mere" hostages receiving a hero's welcome, and compared it to their own return from actual combat in Vietnam.

Implicit in American neglect of the war is a very subtle interpretation of the Vietnam experience with significance both for an understanding of the war, as one event, and for comprehension of the broader trends of American foreign policy. That is, the refusal to confront the war as a massive failure and then the tendency to focus primarily on only certain narrow types of questions seem to represent an unconscious wish to see the Vietnam War and American participation in it as an aberration as far as long-term and worldwide involvement of the United States is concerned.

We need only recall the uproar over United States aid to Zaire in the mid-1970s and the contemplated aid to El Salvador by the incoming Reagan administration in the spring of 1981 to realize the potency of this very implicit argument. The continuing debate in the Reagan administration over United States' involvement in El Salvador and elsewhere in Central America, as well as in Lebanon in the summer and

Competing Perspectives

fall of 1983, constantly focused on analogies to Vietnam. Public support for involvement in all these instances was very difficult to produce. (By contrast, the support for the United States' invasion of Grenada in October 1983 received widespread support in very short order, but there was no public debate beforehand and the effort was viewed as successful.) Americans say they do not want "another Vietnam" to occur. "Mistakes" were made. The United States has "learned its lessons." It will never again allow itself to become involved in such costly ventures. Vietnam and all that it encompasses, both internationally as well as domestically, is over and done with. Involvement in other "possible Vietnams," such as Zaire and El Salvador, is to be carefully guarded against.

But to view the war as an aberration, as something that somehow got out of hand, as evidence of bad decision makers making bad decisions and poor foreign policy, as deceptive politicians misleading the public, is to focus only on narrow domestic factors that handily direct blame to decision makers. President Lyndon Johnson has carried most of the blame in this regard, but President Nixon also received a great deal for continuing the war much longer than many people felt was really necessary. Parenthetically, it is interesting to note that, on balance, not as much blame has been leveled at President Kennedy, who made the first real troop commitment to Vietnam, increasing manpower levels there from 685 advisors to over 16,000.

Blame is also placed on the anti-Communist mania of the containment policy; this "explains" the Vietnam War because decision makers felt they had to combat Communism around the globe, thus justifying intervention in Vietnam (Nacht, 1980). We will see in a later chapter that this calculated reaction to the "Communist menace" does have some validity, and that some evidence can be cited in its favor; but it lacks conviction, and there is other evidence that raises serious doubts about it.

This work, then, derives from a feeling that Americans have not truly dealt with their involvement in the Vietnam experience; instead they have ignored the war, treated it as an aberration that will of course never happen again, or narrowed down the questions asked concerning the American involvement. They have not really grasped either the true complexity of the origins of the Vietnam War and America's participation in it, or the possible consequences of the war. The major goal of this book is to place the Vietnam War and, more broadly, American foreign policy, into several different contextual perspectives. This work is not aimed at finally accounting for the war by piling up numerous different plausible factors and thereby explaining it more fully than by focusing on a single factor. Nor is it an attempt to present a cohesive, tight model or theory of all the factors causing the Vietnam War to take the path it did, or to bring together in a systematic way competing explanations of Vietnam and eliminate some and confirm the strong influence of others.

Methodologically, this work is not, strictly speaking, a case study of a specific war. Instead it takes a specific case study, the Vietnam War, and tries to place it within some general contexts that have been developed by social science theorists to deal with more than one specific case. At the same time, neither is it a true test of any social science theories as social scientists might go about testing them.

In a sense, this work can be seen as an interface between the analysis of a specific case, on the one hand, and the use of social science theories and hypotheses to explore relationships across many cases, on the other. In other words, it is an attempt to apply to a "point-specific" case some of the social science theories in international politics and foreign policy that have been developing for more than a generation. These are not tests or confirmation or proof of the theories or the hypotheses, but are attempts to shed broader light on this specific case using theories and approaches normally applied to a larger number of cases.

Finally, this is not an *apologia* for any of the decisions made by American leaders during the war, many of which *were* bad decisions and were labeled as such by critics of the war. Rather, the primary goal is to increase our understanding of the war by cutting into it—not unlike the way Graham Allison suggests different "cuts" into decision-making in the Cuban missile crisis (Allison 1971)—in several different ways and by placing the war in several different, and sometimes competing, contexts. These distinct contexts should prove enlightening concerning our view of the war in the 1980s and therefore, more broadly, the contours that American foreign policy is likely to follow in the future.

Several other important goals have motivated this work. One is to demonstrate that the study of American foreign policy need not be limited to the traditional diplomatic historian's analysis that makes up the vast majority of the field. Rather, we will show that systematic empirical evidence can be brought to bear on important questions concerning American foreign policy—in the present case, as it relates to American involvement in the Vietnam War. A related goal, as noted already, is to illustrate the relevance of theories of international relations to the analysis of one specific case in United States foreign policy. The goal is not to test any specific theories, but rather to show that there is an alternative to carrying out either one extensive case study with little or no systematic theory or quantitative evidence, or embarking on a highly theoretical and empirical analysis with a large number of cases that then become difficult to relate to any one specific case. At some point we should try to bridge that gap, and this endeavor is a step in that direction.

The several perspectives we have been talking about will be familiar to most. Starting with the most basic unit of analysis, the individual, we will look at changing American perceptions of the war. How much attention was given to the Vietnam situation from the late 1940s through the early 1970s? Was Vietnam always important? Which of those years seemed to be the ones when Vietnam was uppermost in the minds of the American people? Lyndon Johnson was once said to have remarked, in answer to an indirect question on when our involvement in Vietnam began, "Do you want to know how long we've been in Vietnam, son? I'll tell you. We've *always* been involved in Vietnam!" Was this actual, historical fact, or simply the comment of a harassed national leader who by late 1967 was wearying of the war and its increasing toll? Moreover, what implications can we draw from evidence on the attention given to Vietnam?

Second, in terms of the three American presidents most heavily involved in the war, Kennedy, Johnson, and Nixon, how did they define the Vietnam conflict? What was their rhetoric like during the 1961-72 period, and did it change? What were the issues involved, and did those change? We will suggest that the meshing of some social science literature with some fairly simple measures of the presidents' perceptions of Vietnam results in interesting and provocative descriptions of the dynamics of their perceptions as well as the possible relationships of those perceptions to the war.

The next perspective is decision making. Was there a national interest involved in the Vietnam War to which the American decision makers were responding? Was their response a calculated one, designed to achieve the large-scale goal of containing Communism? Or were other factors involved in the decision-making process in Vietnam? How can we best characterize the internal process of decision making on Vietnam? A lengthy debate has raged over how to best describe foreign policy decision making in general (Allison 1971) and, more specifically, in the case of Vietnam. Some argued that nonrational, incremental decision making was involved (Sullivan 1974; Gallucci 1975; Janis 1972); others argued that although that might have been the case in some decisions, nonetheless decision makers by and large "knew what they were doing" (Ellsberg 1972; Gelb and Betts 1979; Berman 1982). The conclusions one comes to concerning the validity of the contending sides in this debate directly influence the implications or lessons to be drawn about the Vietnam War and America's role in it. Some contend that bad, inefficient, or even malicious leaders were the problem, and had other leaders been in office during those times, Vietnam would not have turned out as it did. Many feel, for instance,

Competing Perspectives

that if President Kennedy had not been assassinated in November 1963 the United States would have been able to extricate itself from Vietnam without the excessive commitment later undertaken during President Johnson's term in office. And later, the argument goes, had Hubert Humphrey been elected over Richard Nixon in 1968, the war could have ended much earlier than it did.

But the other side in this debate suggests that decision makers at all times are caught in the cross fire of competing goals and desires of the many individuals and groups involved in the decision making, and that the process of producing good decisions is not solely a function of having good and wise decision makers. In other words, decision making is a complex process that does not correspond to some preconceived set of rules and guidelines for making a good or the best decision.

Going beyond the individual and the decision makers, American foreign policy can be viewed from even broader perspectives. Ideas originally outlined by Frank Klingberg and others suggest that American foreign policy might alternate between moods of introversion and extroversion, and that these different moods, although not directly causing or preventing any given foreign policy action, nonetheless serve as strong background factors, in the context of which specific actions or trends take place. In addition to the types of evidence that Klingberg suggested as illustrations of the fluctuations in the contrasting moods, public opinion polls taken during and after the Vietnam War lend support to such an interpretation. The polls also effectively highlight what the public view of the war was while the early decisions on the war were being made, a view that in some cases is in stark contrast to public attitudes near the end and after the termination of the war.

Finally, we consider the Vietnam War from the perspective of other long-term trends. First we ask, if the American involvement in the Vietnam War was at least partly a function of the larger Cold War, containment, anti-Communist stance of the United States at the time, then in what ways does the war fit into that larger posture? More important, if it does not, then what implications can we draw concerning that argument? To state this differently, one of the questions taken up in chapter 5 is how much effect the overarching perception of the Cold War between the United States and Russia and the necessity and advisability of the containment policy had in terms of producing decisions for further American involvement. We attack the same question not from the perspective of the decision maker's perceptions, but whether the Vietnam War really did fit into that larger U.S.-Russian Cold War and the policy of containment.

Expanding that view even further, we will suggest a perspective that will no doubt strike some as much too broad to be meaningful and much too mechanistic and deterministic to be possible. That is, research has suggested that there is variation in international violence over long periods of time, and that such variation is not a totally random phenomenon. Some evidence going back almost 500 years suggests possible cyclical patterns in international violence, and although there remains much dispute about this evidence, it is too intriguing to ignore. Furthermore, there is also some suggestion that different types of wars occur at different periods of time in the long cycle of international history, and we will see how Vietnam can be related to this long cycle.

This work originally developed out of a desire to see what can be learned about the American involvement in the Vietnam War when stepping back and placing it into several different perspectives, and to illustrate what kinds of questions can be addressed by utilizing systematically collected evidence. The lessons Americans take away from their involvement in that war are of necessity going to be dictated by the historical information brought to bear on it as well as the explicit (or, more often, implicit) model or models that are used to frame the American involvement. Whether consciously or not, the American public as well as policymakers have been drawing lessons from that involvement and one lesson that seems to have taken hold is that the involvement was an aberration undertaken by mistaken, mis-

Competing Perspectives

guided, or evil national leaders. While it is true that we have had very few, if any, wars like Vietnam, and therefore its application to other situations may be difficult, nonetheless the focus on failed policy as a function of aberrant decision making produces an extremely narrowly confined lesson. This work is meant to put that lesson into some competing perspectives on the American involvement.

Although the central focus of this work is the American involvement in the Vietnam War, what follows can just as easily be applied to other American involvements, decisions, and policies of the past, the present, and ideally the future, as well as to the foreign policies of nations in general. This work illustrates the ways we can place broad contexts around specific events and movements in foreign affairs, rather than treating them—as so often is the case—as discrete, independent historical entities. It is hoped this approach provides an enhanced, although not necessarily the best or the only, picture of those events and movements. The concluding chapter draws together overall implications of these different perspectives and presents observations about contemporary and future American foreign policy.

2. Vietnam as Vital: Myth or Reality

One of the most elementary principles in the understanding of any nation's foreign policy is that policy flows from the ideologies of the individual leaders of the moment and their perceptions of the situations they find themselves in. Involved also are the values they bring to the situation, and perhaps their own personal idiosyncracies. In terms of the Vietnam case, it has been argued widely that American involvement in that war grew out of American decision makers' perception that in Vietnam they faced the implacable foe of international Communism, that the onslaught must be stopped there, and if it were not, there would be an inexorable string of Communist victories around the world.

Combined in this argument are two components. The first contends that Vietnam was for a long time after World War II important to the United States, that it was constantly referred to by Presidents Eisenhower, Kennedy, Johnson, and Nixon and their administrations as having been of long-term interest to the United States. Consistent references (especially during the Johnson administration), were made to the "commitment" to Vietnam going all the way back to Eisenhower and perhaps even to President Truman.

The second component of this argument is that there were high-level moral and political issues at stake in Vietnam that transcended political party or ideology. They were issues that pitted the democratic ideology of the United States and the West against the Communist and totalitar-

Vietnam as Vital

ian ideology of the Soviet Union and China. At stake in Vietnam were issues of liberty and freedom and democracy, and the will of both the United States and South Vietnam to keep South Vietnam "free"; ultimately, it became an issue of American pride and honor. This chapter investigates both components, and finds that while both are true to a limited degree, they are also part myth. The very involvement in Vietnam itself has served to color what the objective reality was in the years before and during the actual involvement. It is instructive, then, to look at Vietnam with some systematic evidence concerning two things: (1) how important it was to decision makers at the time and (2) how widespread and lasting the political values alleged to have brought about the involvement actually were.

VIETNAM'S IMPORTANCE

While it may seem odd, given the intensity with which the United States ultimately devoted itself to the prosecution of the Vietnam War and the massive costs it incurred, some indirect evidence suggests that Vietnam was not of constant and intense importance to decision makers throughout the course of the Cold War.

Even raising this question is in a sense baffling, primarily because after the experience of the war itself, it is almost impossible to believe that decision makers did not always have Vietnam uppermost in their minds. They must have! Otherwise, why did such an extensive involvement occur? Indeed, there is little doubt that expressions of concern about Vietnam were present throughout much of the post—World War II period. But the important question is not whether expressions of concern were made, but rather how those expressions compared with the other concerns of United States foreign policy decision makers, and what can be discerned from any possible patterns in those expressions about Vietnam?

Before moving to the evidence to be presented, some assumptions must be made. First, decision makers do not operate in a vacuum, nor do they make decisions so secretly that no one ever finds out what they have done. That is, even if (as we know is the case) decisions are sometimes made in secret, their result will sooner or later surface. Second, decision makers' interests in various issues are transmitted to the public through speeches, press conferences, press releases, leaks, and so on, and the public and the press have a way of gauging what seems to be in the forefront of the minds of the president and other leaders.

To put it simply, it is unlikely that national leaders would be intensely engrossed and concerned about an issue and be able to prevent that fact from becoming known to the press, to the nation's allies and adversaries, and to the public. Presidents do not consult with their closest aides by whispering in dark closets in the basement of the White House with no records of the meetings being kept. It is a very hard thing to hide, especially in the United States where the media are in competition with each other to ferret out every possible piece of information. Although certainly not true in every instance, it is safe to assume that decision makers' interests will usually emerge into the public domain. It is possible to discover what their interests are, and even the intensity of those interests by listening to what they say and what they focus on.

With these assumptions in mind, we can turn to a question that forms a piece of the Vietnam puzzle: what were decision makers really interested in? To find out we need a measure of that interest that cannot be consciously doctored by the decision makers to mislead. It must be an unbiased measure. To ask a government spokesman to provide an "index" of United States' interest in Vietnam and then to rely on that index might be highly inaccurate. Further, to rely on after-the-fact interviews with decision makers, especially long after the fact, would also be potentially misleading. For one thing, those who have been close to the decision making on a given situation can easily overestimate the amount of interest in it. Second, decision makers have been

Vietnam as Vital

known to rewrite history to their advantage. And finally, of course, the problem of faulty memories comes in: eliciting such information years or even decades after the fact could be hazardous in terms of generating reliable empirical evidence. A measure is needed that, in the long run, is unlikely to be tampered with successfully. One such method involves analysis of published sources.

Of the many ways to track what a national leader is interested in, we have chosen to look at the outward and direct contact with the public, and have derived several similar types of measures from different sources. For instance, the annual volumes entitled *The Papers of the President* provide all of the presidential verbal output for the previous year. Included are all of the president's public utterances, from lengthy televised national addresses to the shortest comment in the Rose Garden to a group of Boy Scouts. This source gives a very rough overall view of the amount of attention the president devotes to any given issue, individual, country, or region of the world.

To generate a general picture of the "attention to Vietnam" by the successive presidents, a simple frequency count of the number of page references in the index to *The Papers of the President* to Vietnam and to a number of other countries and regions of the world was undertaken for the years 1946 to 1970. Although the results may not contradict what one would intuitively expect, the picture drawn from this evidence is quite interesting in terms of what, in reality, was going on then.

The data on Vietnam from *Papers of the President* had to be compared to the data on references to other countries. France was chosen for comparison because it was a major European ally of the United States, a powerful country, and had also been involved in Vietnam; Mexico, because it bordered the United States and was relatively close to the United States diplomatically; and Paraguay, because it had little or no strategic importance to the United States. References to Asia were tabulated because even if references to Vietnam were not numerous, one might argue that the commitment was to the broader Asian region. The other countries included were South Korea, Turkey, Laos, El Salvador, Canada, the United Kingdom, China, and Japan. South Korea and Turkey were closely allied with the United States, and small. Canada, the United Kingdom, and Japan were also close allies of the United States, but all were large and developed. Laos was, at least in the early 1960s, in a situation similar to Vietnam's, with an internal conflict raging and the respective sides backed by the opposing superpowers. El Salvador was chosen because, by and large, during the Cold War this small Central American nation was unimportant to the United States; but in 1981, President Reagan and his new administration made decisions on El Salvador that made it take on importance to the United States' strategic posture. China was large, relatively undeveloped through most of the period, and until 1971 was a bitter enemy of the United States.

Table 1 presents the evidence from *Papers of the President.* If Vietnam had been truly important through most of those years, then shouldn't we expect it to receive as much as, and most likely more, attention than all, or at least most, of these countries? Vietnam received no references until 1953 because it was referred to in earlier years as French Indochina. But not until the early 1960s did Vietnam begin to receive substantially more attention than either France or Mexico. Not until 1963 do Vietnam and Asia differ markedly from the other countries in attention received. Asia and France received more attention in 1951 and 1954, but even by 1962 Mexico received more attention than Vietnam and Asia. Only the years 1963 through 1969 for Asia and 1970 for Vietnam, clearly indicate heightened decision maker interest in Vietnam and Asia. By 1974 Paraguay again received just as much attention as Asia, and Mexico was roughly the equivalent of Vietnam in terms of attention received.

It is noteworthy that for the late 1950s especially, China, Canada, and Japan received as much or more attention than Vietnam. El Salvador is the only one of these countries re-

Vietnam as Vital

Table 1. References to Vietnam and to Other Countries in *Papers of the President*, 1946–1970

Year	Viet-nam	Asia	Laos	Para-guay	Japan	Can-ada	Tur-key	PRC	UK	France	El Sal.	So. Korea	Mex-ico
1946	0	8	0	0	49	34	2	85	91	13	0	5	5
1947	0	9	0	0	24	25	33	12	60	25	0	10	26
1948	0	9	0	0	21	24	17	69	32	8	0	4	6
1949	0	12	0	0	12	27	8	54	92	16	0	14	54
1950	0	39	0	0	47	28	12	40	67	34	0	110	15
1951	0	41	0	0	23	16	6	14	36	36	1	27	12
1952	0	40	1	1	20	34	24	6	41	21	0	37	9
1953	2	15	5	0	0	34	0	27	41	20	0	43	8
1954	14	34	5	0	22	13	8	12	40	36	0	44	6
1955	8	17	1	0	0	5	5	22	15	2	0	6	5
1956	7	8	0	0	11	5	3	9	33	19	0	15	4
1957	12	11	1	0	23	14	9	11	41	18	0	2	2
1958	14	9	0	0	11	12	6	28	24	18	0	15	4
1959	5	8	9	0	7	18	29	19	63	53	3	5	24
1960	7	10	8	0	48	12	3	17	35	35	0	53	18
1961	23	29	60	0	21	32	4	32	33	26	1	6	2
1962	34	35	62	0	24	16	6	25	27	32	0	7	40
1963	62	64	59	0	22	14	11	35	91	36	5	24	20
1964	182	43	21	0	15	31	34	38	54	10	0	4	30
1965	320	80	5	0	44	30	3	15	21	8	3	33	10
1966	565	77	7	0	11	10	5	22	22	14	0	48	43
1967	600	69	18	0	23	18	28	15	22	4	1	27	38
1968	465	87	10	5	12	17	6	2	21	12	17	41	23
1969	415	94	14	0	30	23	8	25	32	35	0	40	20
1970	478	41	41	0	18	8	1	3	12	35	0	8	37

ceiving markedly less attention than Vietnam, although in 1956, 1959, and 1960 it is not radically lower than Vietnam. Not surprisingly, the United Kingdom received a great deal of attention. South Korea, Turkey, and Vietnam received equivalent amounts; and the attention to Laos roughly parallels that of Vietnam.

Interpreting such evidence is admittedly subjective, and no one interpretation can be entirely correct. Nonetheless, if the question of concern is "How important was Vietnam to American decision makers?", then this evidence suggests that it was not until the early 1960s, more specifically 1963 and especially 1964, that Vietnam became of overriding importance in presidential concerns. But this is only one piece of evidence, although a highly central one in terms of presidential decision making.

Other evidence, however, basically confirms these find-

Table 2. Pages on Vietnam and on Other Countries in *Britannica Book of the Year*, 1946–1970

Year	Vietnam	Asia	Laos	Paraguay	Japan	Canada	Turkey	PRC	UK	France	El Sal.	So. Korea	Mexico
1946	--	.40	--	1.00	3.00	5.00	1.00	2.00	4.00	3.00	1.00	1.00	3.00
1947	--	.20	--	.75	3.00	6.00	1.00	3.00	4.00	3.25	.50	.50	3.00
1948	--	.25	--	.75	2.00	6.00	1.00	2.00	3.75	3.00	.50	.50	3.00
1949	--	.50	--	1.00	2.00	5.00	1.00	3.00	4.00	3.00	.50	.50	2.50
1950	--	1.50	--	1.00	2.50	3.00	1.00	3.50	4.00	3.00	.50	.50	1.75
1951	--	1.00	--	.80	2.50	2.50	1.25	2.75	4.00	3.00	.50	.50	1.75
1952	--	1.00	--	.50	2.25	2.00	.75	2.50	4.50	3.75	.50	.50	1.50
1953	--	1.25	--	.80	2.50	2.75	1.00	2.25	4.00	3.50	.50	.50	1.50
1954	--	2.25	--	.75	2.50	3.00	1.00	2.50	3.75	3.50	.50	.50	1.25
1955	1.00	1.50	.25	1.25	3.25	2.25	1.25	2.50	3.50	3.25	.75	.75	1.50
1956	.75	1.50	.25	.75	2.50	1.75	1.50	3.25	3.50	3.25	.75	.75	1.00
1957	.75	1.50	.50	.75	2.00	2.25	1.50	2.75	3.75	3.50	.75	.75	1.00
1958	.75	1.50	.50	.75	2.25	3.00	1.25	2.50	3.25	5.25	.50	.50	1.50
1959	1.00	2.50	1.00	.75	2.00	2.50	1.00	2.50	3.25	3.00	.75	.75	1.25
1960	.75	2.25	.75	.75	2.00	2.50	1.00	2.75	3.75	2.75	.75	.75	1.50
1961	.75	2.50	1.25	.75	2.50	2.25	1.50	2.25	3.00	2.50	.75	.75	1.50
1962	2.00	3.00	1.00	.75	2.00	4.00	1.25	2.50	3.00	3.25	.50	.50	1.00
1963	1.75	3.50	1.00	.80	1.75	3.00	1.00	3.00	3.50	2.25	.75	.75	1.00
1964	3.25	5.50	1.25	.75	2.00	8.50	1.75	3.00	4.00	2.00	.50	.50	1.75
1965	4.00	5.50	.75	.75	1.75	5.00	1.25	2.75	3.00	2.75	.50	.50	1.50
1966	4.75	6.50	.75	.50	2.00	3.75	1.25	2.75	3.75	2.00	.75	.75	1.50
1967	4.00	6.00	1.00	.75	2.00	7.00	1.50	3.25	3.50	2.75	.75	.75	1.50
1968	5.75	7.25	.75	.75	2.00	5.00	1.25	6.00	4.25	3.75	1.00	1.00	1.50
1969	5.00	9.75	.75	.75	2.25	4.00	1.50	3.00	4.25	4.00	.75	.75	1.75
1970	4.75	9.00	.75	.50	2.25	7.25	1.00	3.50	5.00	3.50	1.25	1.25	1.25

NOTE: The data under "Asia" refer to the number of pages under "Asia" for 1946–1949; "Indochina" for the years 1950–1954; and are the summation of the pages devoted to Vietnam, Cambodia, and Laos for 1955–1969.

ings. The *Britannica Book of the Year* is another readily available source. We can assume that the editors of this annual volume will reflect in their allocation of space contemporary perceptions of what is going on and where public attention is focused. Table 2 shows the number of pages devoted to the same countries and areas as in table 1. France received the most attention throughout the 1946-74 period, on average, and until 1964 it received more attention than any of the other three countries. From 1952, when it first appeared, until 1954, Vietnam received less attention than Mexico and Paraguay. It again consistently received less attention than Mexico until 1961; and it was not until 1964 that Vietnam became more important than Mexico. Attention to Vietnam relative to Paraguay was roughly equal from 1955 to about 1960. Vietnam earned less than two pages a year until 1964. Throughout that period both Turkey and Korea were viewed as more important. Even El Salvador up until 1960 was seen as almost as important as Vietnam.

Gelb and Betts note that by December of 1964 some advisors in the Johnson administration felt that, after the fall of the seventh government in Saigon, it was a ripe time for reappraisal of United States policy. But, they argue, "LBJ was not about to become the first president to lose a war. And the argument (concerning reappraisal) would have been relevant only if the administration had not genuinely cared about the perceived importance of Vietnam" (1979, 107). Although Vietnam may have been perceived as of some strategic importance, the evidence presented here suggests that before 1964 it was only one of a number of countries of interest to the United States, and perhaps not of major importance.

Now let us turn to a third and related set of evidence. Although the source is quite different, the story that is told is similar. The *Pentagon Papers* was a multivolume work produced by a special task force in the Department of Defense appointed by Secretary of Defense Roberet McNamara in 1966. The goal of the force was to go through the internal documents and published histories since 1945 in order to chronicle the American involvement in Vietnam. Originally meant for internal use only, the papers were ultimately leaked to the *New York Times* by Daniel Ellsberg, a former Defense Department official who had worked on the project, had slowly become disillusioned with the war, and ultimately left government service in protest. The *Papers* contain a wealth of information. A separate edition of the Pentagon Papers was published by Senator Gravel of Alaska; this edition contains some documents not in the *New York Times* edition, and omits some that the *Times* edition includes. The Gravel edition also contains a volume of papers written by academics and others analyzing both the papers themselves and the American role in the war.

Investigating both the *New York Times* edition of the *Papers* and the Gravel edition we find (figure 1) that the pattern of internal official documents on Vietnam conforms to the patterns we have seen already from public sources. That is, little or no attention was given to Vietnam from 1946 to about 1951–52, with a sudden burst of attention in 1954 when the Geneva meeting on Vietnam took place. After the attention of that year, from 1955 through 1959, there is again minimal attention to Vietnam. The first marked increase occurs in 1961, followed by a decline in 1962. It was in late 1961 that President Kennedy dispatched Maxwell Taylor and Walt Rostow to Vietnam to investigate the situation, which resulted in Kennedy's first decision to increase the American involvement in Vietnam. However, despite this, 1962 again shows a decline, at least in the *New York Times* edition, to a level not much above earlier years. A large surge in 1963 and 1964 (with the Tonkin Gulf incident and the passing of the Tonkin Gulf Resolution in the latter year) was followed by a decline through 1968.

As the American involvement increased, decision makers, in addition to paying more attention to Vietnam, felt more and more compelled to justify the involvement. The Gravel edition of the *Papers* presents a count of the number of times American involvement was explicitly justified. The same pattern as that apparent in official documents repeats itself. With the exception of 1954, the entire decade of the 1950s shows a very small number of justifications for American involvement in Vietnam. Not until 1960 do these reappear. Such justifications of the American involvement continue to increase and peak about 1965-66 and then decrease slightly to 1967.

With each of these separate sources of evidence a similar story is told: except for those years in which decisions were being made, Vietnam was not the focus of a great deal of attention. One interesting observation however, which truly runs against what one would have expected to find, is the actual decline in attention to Vietnam in these two sources after 1964, and the decline after 1965 in the number of times Vietnam was officially justified in the Gravel edition.

Figure 1. Pages of Official Documents and Number of Justifications of War in the Pentagon Papers

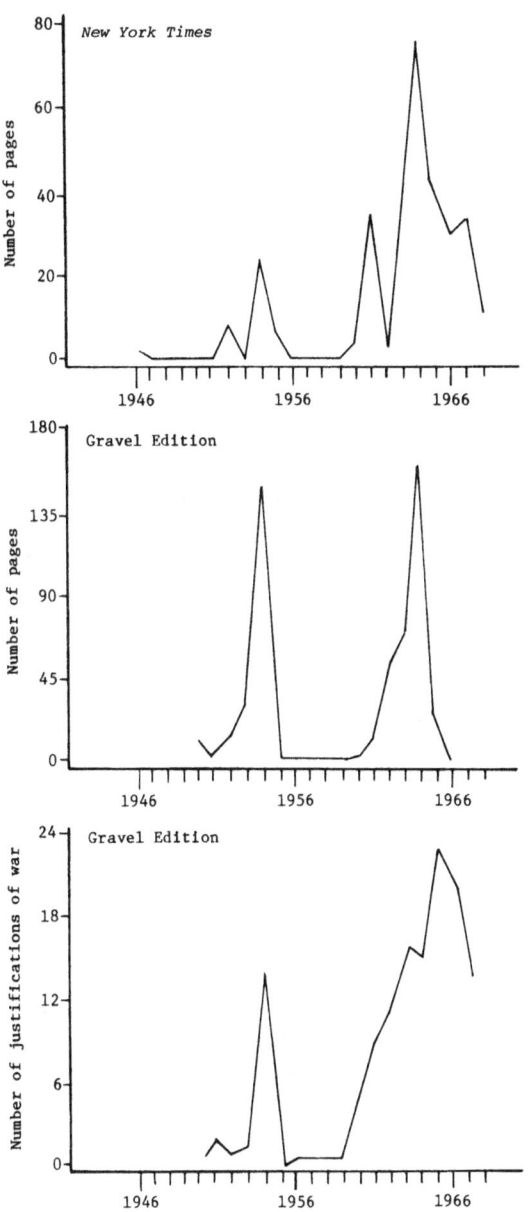

This certainly is an anomaly, for one would have expected, given the pattern of the early 1960s, that the outpouring of documents and justifications for the war would have continued through the late 1960s as the war continued to escalate. This did not happen, almost as if a bureaucratic/military momentum continued the war after the political justifications had brought it about.

The final piece of evidence concerning American leaders' interest in Vietnam relates to the Tonkin Gulf incident in August of 1964 when two American ships, the *Turner Joy* and the *Maddox*, were allegedly fired upon by North Vietnamese boats. President Johnson responded by immediately submitting to the Senate what came to be known as the "Tonkin Gulf Resolution," which was passed 88-2 by the Senate and became Johnson's justification for escalating American involvement in Vietnam. Controversy has surrounded the entire Tonkin Gulf incident since 1964, with the administration at the time arguing that it was an attack on the high seas against American ships, and others contending that the attack was either totally manufactured or at least a result of provocations by the American ships. Some even contend that in one form or another the resolution had been carried around in Lyndon Johnson's pocket for months, awaiting the opportunity some such "incident" would offer.

Resolving that dispute in a satisfactory fashion is probably impossible, since it depends on what one means by saying an incident is manufactured, and exactly what one means by asserting Johnson had the resolution "in his pocket for months." But utilizing the type of evidence presented here, we can reach some preliminary conclusions in an indirect way.

Documents in the *Times* and Gravel editions of *The Pentagon Papers* for 1964 (figure 2) show that March, August, and November are clearly high attention months. Only in those months, especially August and November, when a crisis actually occurred, was there great attention to Vietnam.

We cannot conclude that in fact the Tonkin Gulf was not

Figure 2. Pages of Official Documents in *New York Times* and Gravel Editions of Pentagon Papers, 1964

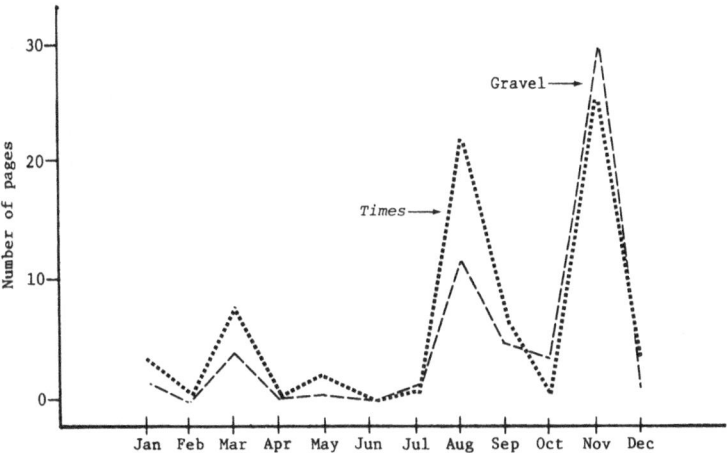

a phony incident; nonetheless, one might suspect that especially in internal documents such as these there might have been greater attention in the four months preceding what many argue was a contrived incident. Here we see April through July recording very low levels of attention. This evidence is not hard and fast, certainly. But nonetheless, whereas we have seen a rising crescendo of attention by year in the earlier evidence, starting in 1961, we do not see the same pattern in the year in which one of the major incidents, that at Tonkin Gulf, occurred.

Admittedly, the preceding evidence has limitations, and rests on several assumptions. One limitation would seem to be its simplicity. In fact that may be a virtue, for because of its unobtrusive nature, it would be difficult for decision makers to doctor, and is also unaffected by our investigation. Interviews with top decision makers involved in Vietnam on the other hand, would be contaminated by the fact that interviews themselves affect the situation: the interviewee naturally wishes to make himself look as good as possible for history, and therefore responses to questions might be colored. For that reason, the simplicity of the data presented here, despite the drawbacks, make it preferable to other types of evidence.

It is impossible to conclude at this point that Vietnam was not what some critics have said it was all along: of constant and primary concern to decision makers as a testing ground of the United States in its battle against the Communist bloc. It is not surprising that as the American involvement there increased, so did the attention to Vietnam and justification for that involvement. What we see here are not shifts from a fair amount of interest to high levels of interest, but rather changes from relatively little attention to great levels of attention. It is unlikely that Vietnam could have been of great and constant importance to decision makers and not show up in this evidence. Seeing what the American perception became (especially by the late 1960s, with Vietnam dominating the daily workings of the foreign policy bureaucracy and justifications for that involvement spewing forth every day), does not mean that we can conclude that such interest was always there and *therefore served as the rationale for that extensive commitment to Vietnam.*

Vietnam, it appears, was of no greater concern than many other countries and it did not become of great interest to decision makers until certain fateful decisions were made to become further involved. Vital or national interests, therefore, may not have brought about the involvement; the involvement may have been a function of decisions made for other reasons, perhaps incremental reasons. There may also have been much larger forces driving decision makers down the general path they took—toward further escalation of the war—rather than toward the opposite path of deescalation and disengagement from the Vietnam situation. These ideas are taken up again in later chapters. American attention to and interest in Vietnam, therefore, was not steady, but rather was dynamic and changing, and perhaps responded as much to the changing situation there as causing it.

SYMBOLS AND THE UNITED STATES COMMITMENT

If attention, as measured by official documents, can be used to answer questions about American foreign policy in Vietnam, analysis of the content of those documents also might be useful. What follows in this section is based on the assumption that the substantive verbal output of politicians is very important. One reason is so many people pay so much attention to what politicians say. While one of the most popular American pastimes is denigrating anything politicians say, nonetheless the media pay a great deal of attention to it, networks analyze it, and every four years an unlimited amount of attention goes into dissecting what the presidential political contenders "stand for." Rhetoric is an important tool, for it persuades, influences, and often serves as a meaningful social indicator. Murray Edelman has suggested that "symbols" may be used for "political" purposes. A politician "may talk about the defense of freedom against Communist aggression from the north in Vietnam, conveying a picture of a gallant, freedom-loving people united in their resistance to a foreign invader. This is the model of reality that legitimizes American military action in Vietnam" (1971, 69). Accusing a foreign government of being "aggressive" has the effect of "creating perception of threat and evoking mass support for a military position" (160). The symbol of "national interest" is very powerful because it constitutes a "totally ambiguous term" in that it can mean anything we read into it, "even though the various meanings are different and often conflicting." This "semantic hollowness," however, makes it all the more potent as a symbol, for "once an official government agency defines a policy as in the national interest, it is endowed with compelling emotional affect" (165).

Certain types of rhetoric, or symbols, then, represent more than mere political rhetoric. They serve both as a shorthand and as reference points. For example, in the 1960s in the United States the term "long-hair" was a derogatory one. "Communist," "liberal," "hippy," have all been potent symbols evoking images in people's minds; and individuals form into groups, and exclude themselves from other groups, often on the basis of symbols. Lasswell considers symbols as part of the political myth, used to justify and explain specific "power" practices: "One obvious function performed by the key symbol is that of providing a common experience for everyone in the state.... Sentiments of loyalty cluster around these terms, and contribute to the unity of the commonwealth" (1965, 13).

Rhetoric, then, is significant, and changes in rhetoric can often be a very important index of social change. Just as changes in the level of attention paid to Vietnam are important, changes in how we perceived Vietnam, or any situation of American foreign involvement, are also important. An interesting illustration, in terms of the Vietnam case, occurred as the war was winding down. Antiwar journalists were pressuring the American press to stop using the term "enemy" in reference to the North Vietnamese and the Vietcong, arguing that by using the pejorative term the newspapers were taking sides in the war. Although many news outlets refused to change, the *Christian Science Monitor* "officially abolished 'enemy' in favor of less emotional terms such as 'infiltrators'" (*Newsweek* June 12, 1972, 78).

Another and perhaps more vivid example of the change of rhetoric in recent years was the sudden deletion of the word "Communist" in reference to the People's Republic of China during the United States-Chinese rapprochement in the early 1970s. For twenty years, that single word had served as perhaps the most powerful ideological reference point for Americans, and for American politicians, in their depiction of China. The sudden demise of the word, most notably its abandonment by President Richard Nixon—who had risen to political prominence in the 1950s partly by virtue of his virulent anti-Communist attacks on both the Soviet Union and China—served as an important indicator of the serious and far-reaching consequences of changing United States-Chinese relations. Not only did the rhetoric change, but the media and the public took great note of that fact. Thus, although it is popular to ridicule and downgrade politicians' "talk," their words are very significant, and serve as salient indicators of changing political perceptions. To replace "Communist China" with "The People's Republic of China" was not an idle slip of the tongue; that small change in wording signalled a massive shift in United States foreign policy, and was not a meaningless change of a few words.

Next we may ask what type of rhetoric should be listened to, in what way, and what can it tell us? Some hints have been given above in the references to symbols and in the literature dealing with the importance of symbols and their relation to political commitment. Nations, like individuals, become committed to issues, and when the issues change, their commitment is likely to change, and the behavior of the nation relevant to the issues may also change.

There are a wide variety of issues. During World War I, for instance, one issue for the United States was "making the world safe for democracy." During the Second World War, a primary issue was the "unconditional surrender" demanded of the Axis powers. When the U.S.S. *Pueblo* was seized by the North Koreans in 1968, the issue was limited to the return of the eighty-three men and their boat; it could have been generalized into one of freedom of the seas, "Communism," aggression, and the "safety of the free world," but it was not. Shortly after the Tet offensive in Vietnam in 1968, Secretary of State Dean Rusk noted that "the issue being tested in Vietnam is credibility" (Graff 1970, 136). Henry Kissinger, writing before becoming a top presidential advisor, noted that the debates on Vietnam were still being conducted along the lines of the early debates of 1961-62. But, argued Kissinger, "the commitment of 500,000 Americans has settled the issue of the importance of Vietnam. For what is involved now is confidence in American promises. However fashionable it is to ridicule the terms 'credibility' or 'prestige,' they are not empty phrases; other nations can gear their actions to ours only if they can count on our steadiness" (1969, 112).

Moreover, these issues that a nation focuses on will form

a crucial part of leaders' rhetoric. What were the "issues" in the Vietnam War? Historical analyses of the American involvement have focused on many. Certainly most analysts would see the major issues conveyed by American leaders to the American public to be a Western defense of "freedom" against "aggressive Communists." Ultimately, American "pride" became wrapped up in the ideological defense of "liberty" and "justice" in Vietnam. Vietnam was seen as one more example of totalitarian tyranny and aggression, not unlike Hitler's aggressive moves in Europe in 1939, the North Korean invasion of South Korea in 1950, and the Russian invasion of Hungary in 1956. It is true that Vietnam did go to war with several of its neighbors subsequent to the United States' departure; but one of those, China, had been thought throughout the war to be one of Communist Vietnam's staunchest allies. Leslie Gelb saw the "code words" or issues justifying United States involvement in Vietnam to be commitment, honor, Munich, credibility, U.S. responsibilities, world order, will, Communism, and aggression (Gelb 1970, 4; Gelb and Betts 1979, 188).

Few would dispute this very generalized picture of the American involvement, but some intriguing questions can be raised that relate to its accuracy. First, were these issues always a part of the political rhetoric on Vietnam, or were there changes throughout the war? Second, is it possible that the promoting of those issues might in some way have contributed to the continuing escalation of the war? If other issues had been focused on, would the process and outcome of America's involvement with Vietnam have been different? These questions are important, for our contemporary understanding and evaluation of the Vietnam involvement would be quite different if we found constant and intense concern over these issues throughout the war as opposed to fluctuating changes, especially if those changes formed a pattern. Our understanding of the war is aided also if we can demonstrate that those changes in the issues may have been related to the changes in the war. In other words, was the United States' commitment to the issues in Vietnam a solid, continuing thing or, as was found with the "attention" measure above, did it go through changes? If changes did occur, did they relate to the war? The first question is primarily descriptive, while the second is more theoretical.

Some intriguing social science theory relates "commitment" and "symbols" to the behavior of an individual, a group, or—as in our case—a nation. For instance, relatively simple issues may become "encrusted with ideological verbiage" and become "harder to resolve through compromise because government officials and public alike tend to regard any withdrawal as a sacrifice of some great principle" (K. Holsti 1966, 277). Broad status issues can be linked to uncompromising behavior, while more specific, tangible issues are linked to compromising behavior (Rosenau 1966). Katz notes that "symbolic patriotism" or "symbolic commitment" would more likely demand war whereas functional involvements leave the decision maker a wider choice of alternatives (1967, 18). Mitchell and Mitchell note: "The extraordinary power of ... symbolic issues is demonstrated by the greater incidence of violence in their resolution than is the case with purely material distributive problems" (1969, 147). Thus, tangible issues should be more conducive to negotiation and cooperative bargaining, and intangible issues to rigid, uncompromising, and perhaps even hostile behavior.

A simple, but telling example from interpersonal relations illustrates the argument. For the young couple at the end of the day, a dispute may arise over one or the other's failure to bring home a grocery item. At that point, the dispute can be easily negotiated and solved; the violater can simply return to the store, buy the bread, and live happily ever after. Or, the chore can be promised for the morning. If either option is accepted by the other party, the compromise has resolved the dispute. What happens, however, if the offender does not offer to return to the store, but vaguely promises to do the chore sometime in the future? The situation, in the partner's eyes, is still not solved, and a symbolic accusation may emerge: "You don't love me enough!"

(This may be done anyway, in which case the accuser might have wanted to start a fight in the first place, and the lack of bread for dinner is only a surface manifestation of underlying tension.)

At this point, the issue will still be negotiable, unless the first party also rises to the symbolic issue, and the dispute becomes one over "love." One cannot negotiate a symbolic issue such as love. Unless the offender can refocus the issue toward the negotiable question of the bread, the behavior of the parties is likely to change. A wife might go home to mother, she could sue for divorce, or she could blast away with the .45 kept in the kitchen closet. Although specifics are certainly different, we have all at one time or another witnessed or been involved in such events. The implication of the foregoing, of course, is that leaders of nations may also become involved in a commitment to a "symbolic" issue, which commitment may alter their behavior toward more noncompromising and possibly hostile behavior.

The theoretical explanation for this link between symbols and behavior takes at least three different forms. First, a decision maker may become psychologically or personally committed to an issue or to the outcome he or she desires in a conflict, a commitment not necessarily rationally generated. We know this happens in interpersonal situations affecting an individual's behavior (Kiesler, 1971), and it is certainly plausible that the relationship holds in international situations as well. Second, the decision maker may consciously utilize this symbolic commitment in a rational process of signalling to an adversary. Such bargaining constitutes the give-and-take between nations; George et al., for instance, propose that one way to make coercive diplomacy more successful is to impress upon the opponent the "asymmetry" in their respective commitments to a conflict or an issue (1971).

Finally, the decision maker may use symbolic issues to garner public support for any behavior he wishes to undertake. Neil Sheehan, in his introduction to *The Pentagon Papers*, contended that Congress, the news media, the citizenry, and even international opinion were regarded from within the United States government during the Vietnam War as elements to be influenced. "The policy memorandums repeatedly discuss ways to move these outside "audiences" in the desired direction, through such techniques as the controlled release of information and *appeals to patriotic stereotypes* (1971, xiii, emphasis added)." Regardless of whether one explanation or all three are correct in a given situation, they all link symbolic commitment with uncompromising as opposed to compromising behavior, and, in a conflict situation, with a higher probability of a violent outcome.

Some empirical evidence supports this hypothesis in international behavior. Pool found "ideological" symbols increased in newspaper editorials in both the London *Times* and *New York Times* during the two world war periods but decreased during peacetime (1970, 74). The appearance of the symbol "democracy" increased from 2% of all editorials in 1914 to 12% in 1918; the next significant increase was near the end of the 1930s, prior to the outbreak of World War II (Pool 1970, 150). Pool also notes that in World War II, the big spurt of attention to democracy came before the outbreak of fighting (1970, 216).

In comparing six years of the Vietnam War to the Cuban Missile Crisis and the crisis leading to World War I, it was found that during the 1961-66 period in Vietnam, presidential documents and *New York Times* editorials shifted from concern over "functional" commitments to more "normative" and "symbolic" commitments, and from specific security and territory issues to concern over "status." In the 1914 crisis, attention in the early part of the crisis was on the "initiating incident" of the assassination, but during the high stress period much more attention was given to "symbolic" referents. This did not occur, however, during the Cuban Missile Crisis, where there was consistent emphasis on the initiating incident, the missiles in Cuba (Sullivan, 1972a).

An early study of the Vietnam War limited to Lyndon

Johnson's years showed that although the moving average trend of Johnson's symbolic commitment was negatively related to the trend of the war for the entire 1964-68 period, rather strong relations emerged when separate periods were broken out for analysis (specifically, 1964-66 and 1967-68) (Sullivan 1972b). A later study (a small part of which forms the present section of this chapter) extended that analysis to include the entire 1961-73 period, covering Kennedy, Johnson, and Nixon. It found that increased attention was given to symbolic issues prior to and during the escalatory periods, while decreases in that attention preceded the deescalation of the war (Sullivan 1979). Thus there is both theoretical and empirical support for the hypotheses linking symbolic commitment with violent, as opposed to nonviolent, behavior.

The hypothesis is a general one and can be applied to and tested in international as well as interpersonal relations to assess its scientific validity. It also can be used in the Vietnam case to indirectly answer the first question noted above: was the United States' commitment to Vietnam real in some objective sense and constant and consistent throughout America's involvement with Vietnam, and therefore did American behavior merely flow from that commitment? Or did a posterior rationalization occur? In a more general sense, this question also relates to the larger issue of whether goals and values precede action. The "rationalized" model of decision making, to be investigated in Chapter 3, sees individuals first setting out their goals and then going through a systematic delineation of all the possible alternatives, settling on the one that appears to be more suitable for the given goal. Others see the process in reverse. "Objectives and actions are chosen and values then called upon to justify them . . . this belated reference to ideology often appears as an afterthought . . . when the need arises to enlist public opinion in support of policy" (Levi 1970, 8).

Symbolic commitment or the utilization of symbols to justify large actions thus may be brought into play after decisions have been made. "To a very significant degree ideologies are certainly the consequence, rather than the independent cause, of how the game is played. Men constantly create them to rationalize their behavior. They nonetheless become potent symbols once they are in existence, supplying gratifications, affect, and a justification for militancy on both sides" (Edelman 1971, 160). Specifically in terms of Vietnam, three British journalists, in their work on the 1968 American presidential campaign, suggested that this was the case. "One of the most important political points about America's war in Vietnam was that to an unusual degree, involvement preceded rationale; the war was well advanced before there was any structured national debate about its purpose" (Chester, Hodgson, and Page 1969, 22, 28).

Thus, there are several questions to be asked. If "rhetoric" and "symbols" and the "commitment" to both are important indicators to watch, were there changes in these during the Vietnam War? If changes did occur, how did those changes relate to the war? Finally, can any assessment be made concerning a possible posterior rationalization about the Vietnam War?

Investigating these questions raises some of the same problems noted in the previous section: we could ask the decision makers involved but the answers would be colored. Our method takes off from Murray Edelman's distinction between "condensation" and "referential" symbols. Edelman defines condensation symbols as those that "evoke the emotions" and "condense into one symbolic event, sign, or act patriotic pride, anxieties, remembrances of past glories or humiliations" (1964, 6). Referential symbols are "economical ways" of referring to some "objective elements" in the world. This distinction is helpful because condensation symbols are equivalent to what we call a "symbolic commitment," namely, one involving emotions, patriotic pride, and so on. For our purposes, then, these types of condensation symbols would constitute a symbolic commitment.

Our decision to focus on condensation symbols, therefore, flows from two factors. First, these most clearly represent "symbolic commitment," the notion of a symbol representing patriotic pride, past glories, humiliations, and so on. Second, early attempts to measure the counterpart, the referential symbols, proved to be virtually impossible. It was discovered that such referential symbols were much more difficult to measure and code than condensation symbols, and therefore the decision was made to stay with the latter.

An early precoding of a small number of presidential documents on Vietnam by four coders instructed merely to extract what they felt were condensation symbols produced agreement on numerous symbols such as "aggression," "national interest," "freedom," "democracy," and so on. After further discussion about condensation symbols, symbolic commitment, and the specific symbols extracted, thirty-two symbols were selected. Earlier work on symbols (White 1951; Lasswell 1949; Pool 1970) also used many of these thirty-two and hence they were felt to have value as general symbols not necessarily dependent on specific situations.

In addition, recall the code words for American involvement mentioned earlier by Leslie Gelb: commitment, honor, Munich, credibililty, U.S. responsibilities, world order, will, Communism, and aggression. Six of those nine code words were included in the thirty-two symbol list. Moreover, this research was undertaken in the 1970-73 period. Five years later two of the symbols in the original list had become central issues around which President Carter appeared to be structuring his foreign policy, namely "human rights." Thus, while there will always be some dispute about the generality of any list of symbols, the present list certainly has relevance to the issues concerning American involvement in Vietnam, and are clearly representative of symbols used in many other issue-areas.

Using this 32-word symbol list, all presidential documents on Vietnam appearing in *Papers of the President* from 1961 to January 1973, the period of the major American involvement, a total of 726, were coded, excluding those with less than 100 words. One measure of symbolic commitment consists simply of the frequency of these 32 symbols as a ratio to the total amount of material coded on Vietnam in each quarter. A second measure is to take a ratio of this first

Vietnam as Vital 35

SYMBOLS USED TO CONSTRUCT SYMBOLIC-COMMITMENT INDEX

aggression	liberty
allies, allied	loyalty
cause	national interest
challenge	obligation
commitments, -ed	patriotism, -otic
Communism, -ist	peace, -ful
courage, courageous	prestige
democracy, democratic	pride, proud
determination, -ed	principles
enemy, enemy forces	responsibility
equality	rights
freedom, free, -ly	security, secure
honor, honorable	loyalty
humanity, humane	self-determination
independent, -ence	threat, -ened
justice, just	values
	will, willingness

measure to the total output on all issues. Each measure tells us something a little bit different. The first simply gives us the amount of symbolic rhetoric involved in the Vietnam situation—the number of symbols per unit of attention to Vietnam alone. The second measure takes that first measure as a ratio to the total presidential output per unit of time, in other words, how symbolically important is Vietnam relative to the other concerns the president may have.

These symbols measure the emotional and ideological commitment of the respective presidents to the Vietnam situation. But a symbolic commitment is also a broad and general one as opposed to a narrow one, which relates to the perception of the scope of the conflict. The scope of a conflict may be geographic: conflicts viewed as narrow and limited in scope would be seen as relevant to only a small number of countries or areas of the world, whereas a broad conflict would be seen as relating to and having ramifications for a large number of countries or areas of the world. If one were to find, for instance, that in statements about Vietnam, decision makers mentioned only the United States and North and South Vietnam, one could conclude that their perception of the situation was more restricted and narrow in scope than if they referred to other countries. If a decision maker were to assert, for instance, that the Vietnam conflict had relevance for Thailand, Cambodia, Laos, the Philippines, and ultimately Australia and New Zealand, the perception of the scope of that conflict would be quite different than if the decision makers were to see it as limited to Vietnam only.

Given these assumptions, a frequency count was made of each reference to twenty-five countries and nine regions of the world that had appeared with some frequency during the precoding. These were then used to construct two measures. The first, "Country Reference," was simply the total number of references to all of those countries per quarter divided by the total length of all documents per quarter. The second meaure, called "Scope," was a count, from zero to 34, of how many of those countries or areas had received at least one reference during the quarter. Thus Country Reference measures the total number of references to all countries or areas, while Scope measures how geographically widespread the references to countries or areas were.

There is, of course, no way of knowing whether a decision maker is truly committed to the symbols used, or even believes in them, or knows what they mean. Nor do we know for sure that mention of more and more countries means the decision maker sees the conflict as having broadened in scope. But whether the presidents really believed freedom and justice were at stake in South Vietnam is for present purposes irrelevant, for what we are looking for is any evidence of the changes in the level of that commitment. Moreover, it is reasonable to conclude that a decision maker's reference to more and more countries means he was perceiving any given situation as having more and more relevance to larger parts of the world, and therefore becoming broader in scope.

Figure 3. Quarterly Average of Presidential Rhetoric in Documents on Vietnam

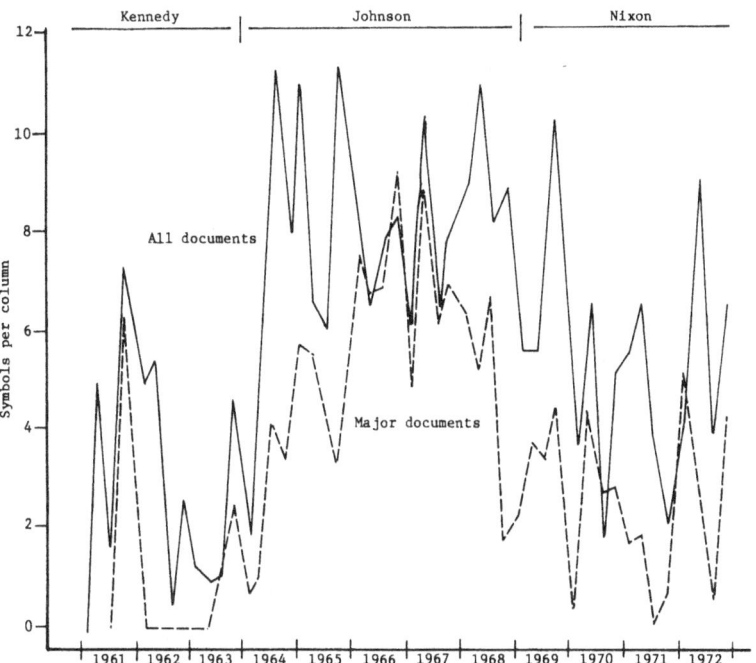

NOTE: Presidential rhetoric is defined as the number of symbols (as listed on page 35) per column of Vietnam documents in *Papers of the President*.

SYMBOLIC RHETORIC: EVIDENCE

Figure 3 shows the quarterly average of symbolic rhetoric from 1961 to 1972 (the last quarter of 1972 includes January 1973) appearing in all documents and in major documents, defined as at least 40% devoted to Vietnam and at least one column in length in *Papers of the President*. It is clear that the more stable measure is the one limited to major documents. In that measure there are no noticeable shifts in the level of symbolic rhetoric across the two changes in administrations, although there is a slight downward movement from Kennedy to Johnson.

For all documents, the fluctuations are generally greater on a quarter-to-quarter basis, since the measure can be greatly affected by a few symbols appearing in several short documents. Even here, however, the larger shifts occur not between administrations but usually within administrations. It is not particularly easy to pick out the change from one administration to another, especially in major documents, and therefore we can track these measures regardless of the individuals involved. (An extended analysis of interpresidential similarities and differences was done in 1982 [Sullivan, 125-46].) This finding of fairly little interadministrative shifting—at least compared to intra-administrative—has a theoretical implication: incremental decision making (to be considered in Chapter 3) would find some support here. In other words, there may be a certain level of rhetorical baggage that passes from one administration to another, baggage that may affect decision making in the receiving administration.

Changes, however, do occur over the twelve years under consideration. Neither measure is flat, nor does either exhibit complete randomness. Focusing primarily on the major documents, we see an interesting pattern. The first surge upward occurred during the last quarter of 1961, which was also when President Kennedy dispatched Maxwell Taylor and Walter Rostow to Vietnam to assess the situation there, the first of many such high-level missions to Vietnam to occur over the next twelve years. It should be noted that it was also during that last quarter of 1961, after Taylor and Rostow returned, that Kennedy made some of the early decisions (in retrospect, very major decisions) to increase American involvement by sending substantially more advisors and troops to Vietnam. A general decline followed through late 1962 and early 1963, but then came a slight increase in late 1963.

What is most interesting, however, occurs during Johnson's years. By the first quarter of 1965, about fifteen months after Johnson took office, an upward trend in symbolic rhetoric had begun, and this continued in a saw-

Vietnam as Vital   39

toothed action to peak about late 1966 and early 1967. From there Johnson's level of rhetoric slowly declined until the last quarter of 1968, when it was at about the same level as in mid-1964. But clearly this shift in Johnson's symbolic commitment was not random: there was a clear tendency for his symbolic commitment to rise during the first three to three and one-half years of the period and then decline for the next twelve to eighteen months. Moreover, Nixon picks up just about where Johnson leaves off, increasing slightly into late 1969, and then proceeding on a somewhat random path through late 1972, with high points in the second quarter of 1970 (Cambodian invasion), first quarter of 1972 (mining of Haiphong harbor and widened air war), and the last quarter of 1972 (massive United States bombing of North Vietnam).

At this point we can conclude that there were changes in the symbolic rhetoric of the presidents and their perception of the Vietnam situation from 1961 to 1973. Thus, to return to the previous section, one could dredge up references to Vietnam from almost any year in the post-1945 period, and one could also find references to such symbols as "freedom" and "democracy" throughout the 1961-73 period. But the evidence presented here suggests that during this latter period the level of rhetoric went through clearly marked shifts. Vietnam was not viewed throughout those years as a constant and vitally important symbolic issue to the presidents.

The most marked and patterned change begins in the second quarter of 1963, with a score of about zero. The symbolic content then escalates clearly over the next three and a half years, peaking out at a score of over 9.0 symbols per column. Then almost an exact reversal sets in, again, for almost three and a half years, and the symbols per column score by the first quarter of 1970 has dropped to just slightly above the 1963 score. In other words, there was a change over almost seven years in the extent of symbolic rhetoric the presidents used with reference to Vietnam; it was not steady, even, constant, and continuous. One can thus doubt the constancy of America's commitment to the symbols that were talked about during the Vietnam War.

What happens to the geographic scope of the conflict during the same period? This measure also goes through marked and patterned changes.

Recall that there are really two measures of the geographic scope of the conflict. The first, Country References, is a count of the times twenty-six countries and nine regions of the world are mentioned. If Laos were mentioned three times, for instance, it would be coded three separate times. In the second measure, Scope, a count was made only if the country was mentioned regardless of the number of times, providing us with a measure of the perceived breadth of the conflict.

Figures 4 and 5 present this evidence. Figure 4 contains country reference data from 1964 to mid-1971, the most active period of the war. It clearly shows an increase in late 1964 and early 1965, followed by a decline in the second quarter of 1965. From that point there is a continuing increase with two setbacks, for the next seven quarters, into mid-1967. The measure then retreats for three quarters, until it again surges into late 1968. From that point the measure declines in early 1969, rises into the first quarter of 1970, and then declines in 1971 to levels the same as 1964. This tracking of the war is not perfect (a question we return to shortly); but the number of references to countries in Vietnam documents is, relatively speaking, low during the early parts of the conflict, surges as the war escalates, and then begins to retreat as the war starts to de-escalate.

Figure 5 presents the evidence on the perceived scope of the conflict. These data span the entire 1961-72 period, and present a picture not dissimilar to that of figure 4. Few countries, relatively speaking, are referred to up until about mid-1965. In that year and the following, the number of countries referred to increases anywhere from two to four times the number of countries referred to in the earlier years. This measure peaks in mid-1966, declines into 1968 and 1969, hits a second peak in 1970, and then again declines by 1972 to the levels of the early 1960s. In both cases

Vietnam as Vital

Figure 4. Trends in Country Reference and U.S. Casualties, 1964–1971 (Country Reference Leading by Three Quarters)

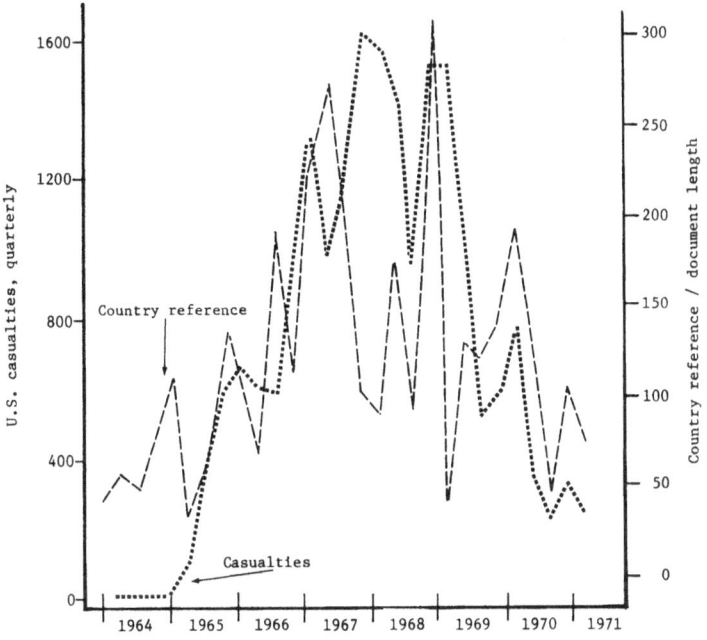

SOURCE for figures 4, 6, and 7: Michael P. Sullivan, Foreign Policy Articulations and U.S. Conflict Behavior. In *To Augur Well: Early Warning Indicators in World Politics*, ed. J. David Singer and Michael Wallace. Beverly Hills: Sage, 1979. Reprinted by permission.

NOTE: Country reference is the total number of references in a given document to 26 different countries and 9 regions of the world, controlled for the length of the document. The curve for casualties is chronologically correct; the country reference data are plotted three quarters earlier than actual occurrence.

it is clear—assuming this measure reflects a perception on the part of the decision makers concerning the scope of the conflict—that the perception of the conflict went through perceptible shifts.

Moreover, these shifts are not random; they are related to the pattern of the war, in particular the pattern of casualties. The Country Reference measure correlates at .47 with the fluctuations in United States casualties in the war, and the Scope measure at .36. Moreover, with both measures, the correlations remain high when the geographic

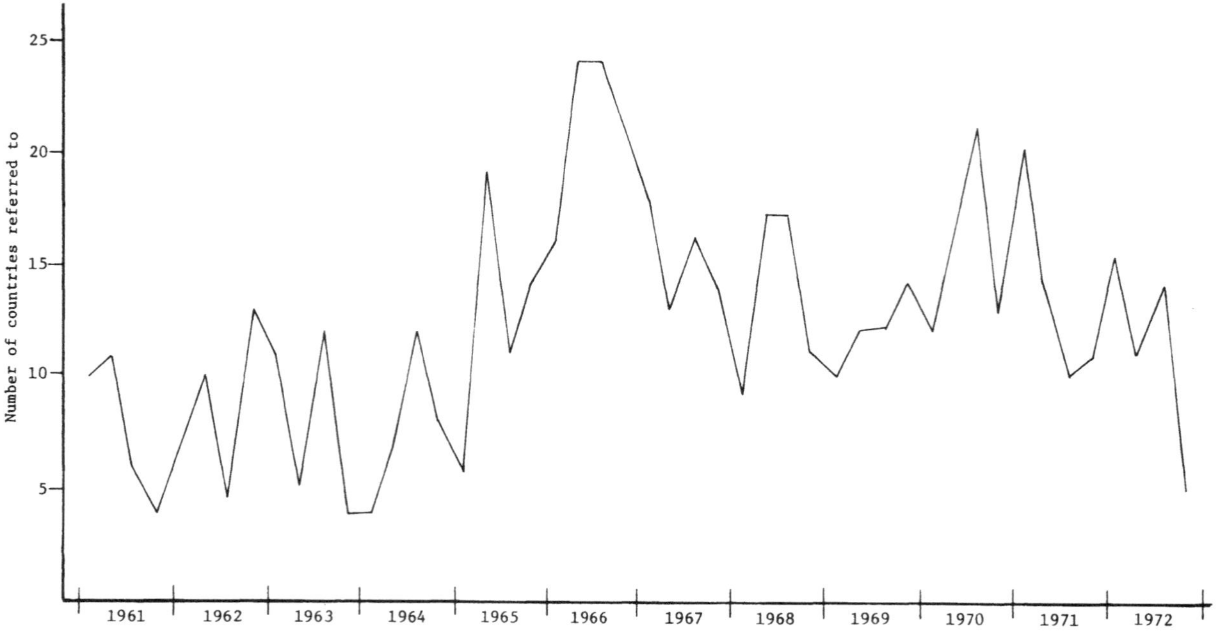

Figure 5. Perceived Scope of the Vietnam War as Reflected in Presidential Documents, 1961–1972

measures are allowed to "lead" the casualty measure in time, while they uniformly drop when casualties are allowed to be the lead indicator (Sullivan 1979, 228). An intriguing relationship is seen by referring to figure 4, which, along with the Country Reference measure, includes the fluctuations in United States casualties; in this case the Country Reference measure is leading casualties by three quarters, or nine months. Clearly the two measures are fluctuating in tandem, with some exceptions during the middle of the series. Country Reference, therefore, might in fact serve as a very good "lead indicator" of escalating conflict. The main point, of course, is that the perception of the conflict changed throughout the course of the conflict. In the present case, as the war intensified and the American involvement broadened, the perception by decision makers of the war broadened in terms of geographic scope: it more and more became portrayed as of great consequence for more and more countries. In fact, figure 4 suggests that this perceptual shift may have begun to occur slightly before the actual behavioral escalation intensified. In other words, the war was not perceived throughout this period as of great consequence for large numbers of countries; these perceptions underwent shifts related to the changes in American involvement in the war.

This evidence suggests clearly that the perceptions of the Vietnam War by the three presidents most heavily involved changed, and that these changes are not unlike the overall "attention" measure presented earlier. It is incorrect to say that the American perception of the Vietnam involvement was a steady, single, constant, commitment to freedom, honor, justice, peace, will, pride, and the other symbols that were called upon to justify American involvement in the war, or that it was consistently perceived as a conflict of worldwide importance.

A question raised earlier, which can be treated only briefly here, relates to the possible relationship between these changes in the level of symbolic commitment and the perception of the scope of the conflict, on the one hand, and

Figure 6. Quarterly Level of U.S. Casualties and Symbolic Rhetoric in Presidential Documents, 1961–1972

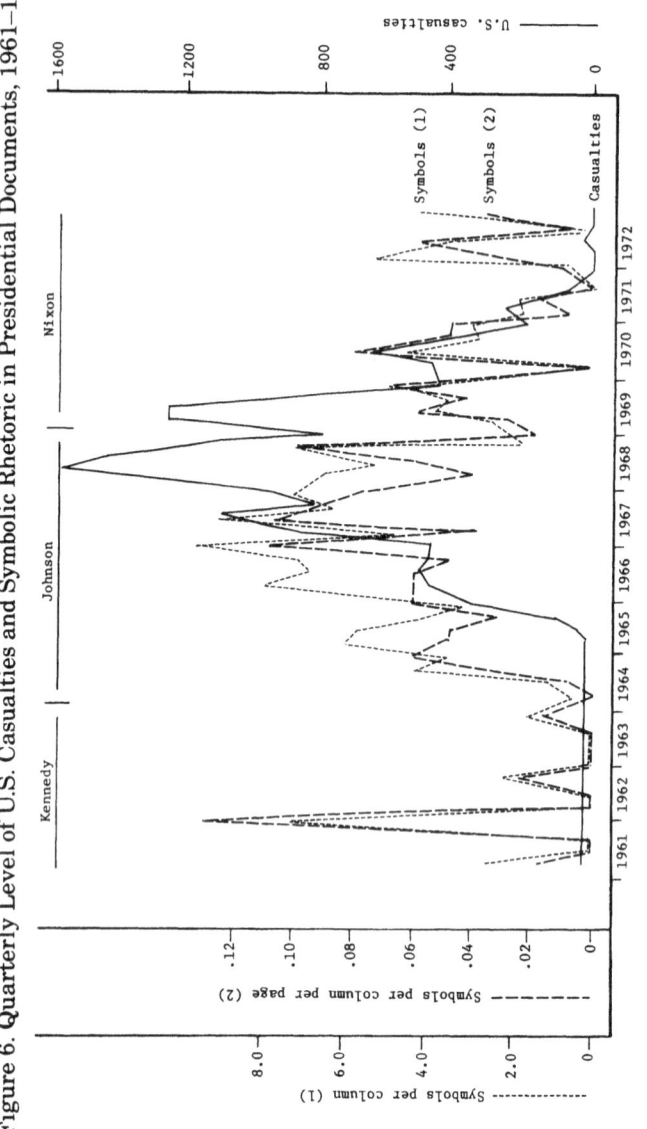

SOURCE: See figure 4.

NOTE: Symbolic rhetoric is measured by counting occurrences in presidential documents of the symbols listed on page 35; "symbols per column" refers to columns of Vietnam documents in *Papers of the President*; "symbols per column per page" is the first ratio divided by the total pages of presidential documents for the quarter.

Vietnam as Vital

the escalation and then de-escalation of the war on the other. An extensive analysis has been presented elsewhere (Sullivan 1979). Figure 6 shows the closest relationship that emerges between symbolic rhetoric (measure 1) in major documents and United States casualties (probably the best short-term measure of American involvement). The changes noted previously in symbolic rhetoric track fairly well with the pattern of the war, with as much as 30% of its variation in common with the level of United States involvement in the war. It is clear from figure 6 that the pattern of symbolic rhetoric and the occurrence of casualties move together. As the war escalates (as measured by casualties), the rhetoric rises. As the rhetoric decreases the war de-escalates. While not a perfect fit, the indicators are not independent.

Another question raised earlier was, what came first, the rhetoric and commitment, or the behavior? It is difficult to answer this for a number of reasons, but by and large when we permit each of the variables to precede the other variable (that is, we lag one variable behind the other), the two phenomena move closer in tandem with each other when the symbolic rhetoric leads; this means that the rhetoric changes first followed by changes in the pattern of United States' casualties.

Figure 7 presents the most telling of these patterns, which occurred during Johnson's administration, when the major escalatory and very early de-escalatory decisions were made. This figure superimposes Johnson's symbolic rhetoric over United States casualties with symbolic commitment leading by three quarters. The trend upward in rhetoric began nine months prior to the upward trend in casualties—roughly the amount of time one would expect decisions to prosecute the war to be translated into final battlefield action. It was also nine to twelve months before American active involvement in the war peaked that rhetoric peaked, which would also fit with what we now know concerning Johnson's growing doubts about the war in late 1967 and early 1968. In addition to the many historical accounts of Johnson's doubts, which led to his famous March

Figure 7. Quarterly Trend in Johnson's Symbolic Rhetoric and U.S. Casualties (Casualties Lagging by Three Quarters)

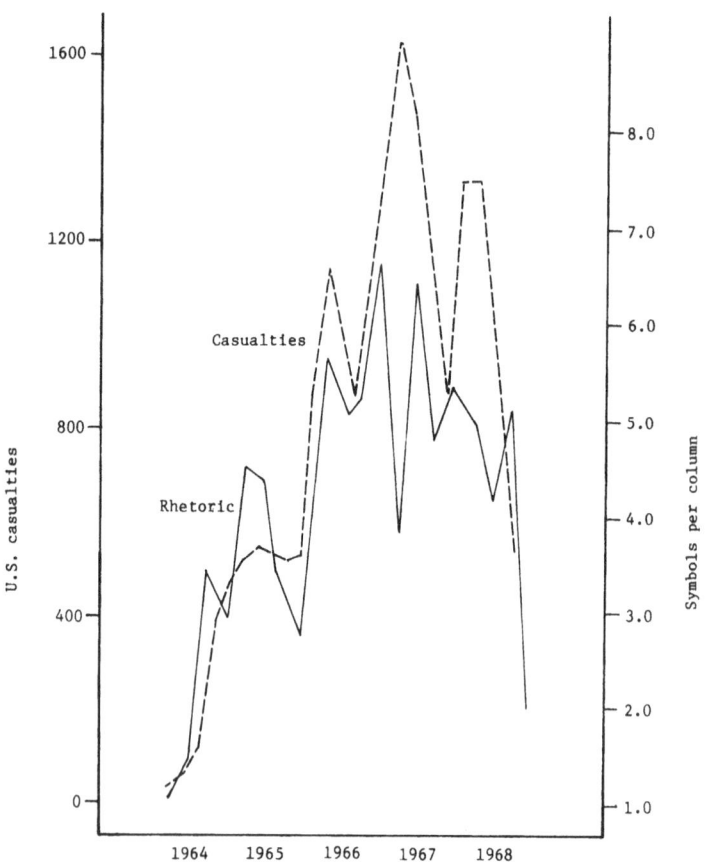

SOURCE: See figure 4.

NOTE: The symbolic rhetoric curve (symbols per column of Vietnam documents in *Papers of the President*) is chronologically correct; the casualties data are plotted three quarters later than actual occurrence.

1968 speech, Miller and Sigelman also show that from August 1967 to March 1968 there was a systematic decline in hawkishness in Johnson's speeches (Miller and Sigelman

Vietnam as Vital

n.d.). They conclude that it was not suddenly in late March 1968, that Johnson reversed the war, but that growing doubts over at least a six-month period had preceded that decision.

Was there then a posterior rationalization in the Vietnam War, or did the commitment to the war precede it and become one of the factors bringing about its escalation? While the best single correlation occurs when the United States' involvement measure is lagged three quarters (or nine months), we still cannot finally conclude that rhetoric occurred first and perhaps caused the war to escalate. The primary reason for this is that, as noted, there is a lag between when the actual decisions are made and when the actual battlefield casualties increase or decrease. Nonetheless, the symbolic rhetoric measure certainly might prove to be a good early indicator of the change taking place in an administration's position and could possibly forecast its future behavior.

This chapter has argued that Vietnam became a truly important public issue only as decision makers began to make decisions concerning United States' involvement. In a sense this is not surprising, for most of us do that most of the time. Yet it also suggests that only after certain decisions were made—and the next chapter will suggest that not all the decisions need be key ones to have an important impact—did decision makers and the public focus on Vietnam and begin defining it as of high symbolic import.

This chapter has also suggested the possibility that symbolic commitment may be a very important social indicator, signalling the trend in the mood of national leaders and perhaps in the country at large. For the United States' involvement in Vietnam, that mood was one of increasing symbolic content as the war was escalating and of decreasing symbolic content as direct American casualties began to decrease. While it would be going too far to conclude that the presidents' growing or decreasing symbolic commitment caused the pattern in the war, it may at least constitute an indicator of the type of policy decisions made at the time. It also may serve to perpetuate and foster further escalation. Escalatory decisions may be easier when symbolic commitment is high or increasing. Such rhetoric is therefore not a random or meaningless phenomenon; it is dynamic, it changes, and certainly bears close watching as a political indicator.

Three possible theories were presented earlier to explain the link between such symbolic rhetoric and violent, escalatory, and nonnegotiable behavior. The first suggested that decision makers actually became committed to the symbols they used, and felt that the Vietnam War did in fact involve questions of democracy, freedom, liberty, justice, and so on, and that such a solid ideological commitment resulted in their further involvement. The second theory suggested that the use of such symbols was an attempt to communicate to the adversary the intensity of interest in this issue, hoping this would force that adversary to back down. The third theory was similar, but on the domestic level: use of such symbols was an attempt to rally the public around the administration's actions in Vietnam.

It is not possible to say here which of these theories is the most accurate. That is, we cannot tell whether the decision makers actually became personally committed to the many rhetorical symbols they used to define the war, and whether they really felt that Vietnam was a true test of "democracy," "will," and "freedom," or that it truly constituted a case of "Communist aggression." Nor can we infer from these data that they were only using these symbols to rouse the public in favor of their policies. Finally, we cannot tell whether the symbols were an attempt to communicate to the North Vietnamese, the Russians, and the Chinese that the American commitment was a vital one.

But from the present perspective it is not necessary to determine which explanation is most nearly correct, because we are trying to indicate the possible importance of the phenomenon of symbolic commitment as a dynamic political indicator. At the same time, thinking now about the

Vietnam as Vital   49

third explanation presented above, we can suggest that just as decision makers and the public realize their own mood is a dynamic, changing one, the same suggestion can be made about an adversary. Just as a decision maker might utilize symbolic rhetoric in an attempt to influence an adversary, so also might that decision maker read the intentions of an adversary in an international conflict by analyzing his use of such rhetoric. In the present case, North Vietnamese rhetoric may have followed similar patterns as U.S. rhetoric and U.S. decision makers might have tried to read the North Vietnamese in terms of their level of symbolic rhetoric to assess the seriousness with which they viewed the situation. In other words, political rhetoric, whether it be one's own or an adversary's, is not merely rhetoric; there is always political rhetoric and it is important insofar as it changes.

The evidence presented in this chapter has suggested that several processes going on during the American involvement in Vietnam were dynamic, and that important changes occurred in those processes that perhaps not only signalled changes in decisions or perceptions, but perhaps might have also played a role in the type of decisions being carried out. While we should not overdraw the implications from this evidence, nonetheless we can speculate that, if President Johnson, his staff, aides, and cabinet members had attempted to define the Vietnam situation in a less symbolic sense, or had begun to defuse it once they realized what was happening, then the pattern of the war might have been different. We are all familiar with conflicts even on an interpersonal level that get out of hand because issues are defined symbolically ("love" rather than a loaf of bread), and neither party is willing to back down. The same process occurs with national leaders and nations. Moreover, the implications do not apply solely to specific international crises, conflicts, or wars, but also to more broadly conceived trends in foreign affairs. For instance, Townsend Hoopes argued that President Kennedy's 1961 inaugural address "was to prove a harbinger of his steady efforts to reduce the moralistic tone of United States foreign policy set by Dulles."

Hoopes argues that Kennedy wanted to view the world through "lenses less tinged with ideology and (problems) could thus be approached with a greater reasonableness by both sides" (1967, 13).

Much later, in the late 1970s, many observers raised serious doubts about the advisability of President Jimmy Carter defining foreign policy issues in terms of human rights, and questioned whether that did not presage a shift to a more moralistic tone in American foreign policy. It is of interest that at just about that same time the policy of détente with the Soviet Union began to erode, followed in 1979 and 1980 by the invasion of Afghanistan by Russia and the internal turmoil in Poland. This strained almost to the breaking point the basically amicable United States-Russian relations of the early 1970s. This link is an illustrative one, of course, but it does point up the possible importance of shifts in political rhetoric that can affect international rivalry, and that may have played a role in the ongoing Vietnam War.

3. Decision-Making Models: Rational Policy or Quagmire?

A central question for policymakers, those studying the policy process, and the public alike revolves around how foreign policy elites make their decisions. How do nations manage to get involved in disputes? How are policies formulated? What goals prompt policymakers to make what decisions?

Perhaps nowhere has the centrality of these questions been brought to bear more urgently than with the Vietnam War, given the fact that it has generally been considered a failure and a mistake, and given the grave costs incurred. The titles of some works about the war reflect disillusionment and distrust: *The Quicksand War* (Bodard 1967), *The Making of a Quagmire* (Halberstam 1965), *No More Vietnams?* (Pfeiffer 1968), "Tonkin Bay: Was There a Conspiracy?" (Scott 1970). These writers and others wonder if we were somehow betrayed by bad decision making.

Several perspectives can be taken on decision making, as we noted earlier, and we can briefly reiterate here two generalized ones specifically relevant to the Vietnam case. First, somewhere, someone, at some time, consciously made long-range decisions that involved the United States in the Vietnamese situation. These decisions resulted from long-range goals perceived as of great importance to the United States. The decision-makers knew the possible consequences, but decided that the risks were made necessary by the importance of the goals. Had other decision makers been there, it is implied, the Vietnam involvement could have been drastically different. Some, for instance, contend that had President John Kennedy not been assassinated in 1963, Vietnam would have turned out differently.

A second view asserts that the policy unfolded in a series of decisions that leaders unwittingly stumbled into. Minor decision piled on top of minor decision until soon Vietnam had become something no one had foreseen or wanted. It had become a monster that no one individual or group had accurately predicted, except perhaps for the very small number of critics of the early decisions, who were viewed at the time as mistaken and perhaps a bit weak.

These two perspectives, in addition to their obvious relevance to our evaluation of the Vietnam case, have much broader implications for decision making in general, and hence for our understanding of United States foreign policy. The following section elaborates on these two decision-making models. They are not new, as the reader will see, but setting them out in partial competition with each other helps us evaluate the decisions on Vietnam. No definitive answers can be given here concerning the validity of one over the other because the type of historical evidence we must rely on can be used to support more than one proposition.

Theodore Draper notes, for instance, that two of the so-called Kennedy historians, Arthur Schlesinger and Ted Sorenson, cite Kennedy's speech of 6 April 1954 against unilateral United States intervention as the "key" to Kennedy's later decisions of 1961, but that neither "recalls the more bellicose pro-French Kennedy of March 9, 1954" (1967, 50). Much of the post-Vietnam criticism of Lyndon Johnson focuses on his bellicose speeches during the war, but fails to remember that he was against supporting the French at Dien Bien Phu in 1954 and was skeptical about any American involvement at the time (*Reporter* 1954, 31-32).

Jonathan Schell, in his critique of United States decision makers for having involved themselves in Vietnam, asserts

Decision-Making Models 53

that decision makers knowingly did what they did because of their preoccupation with the Cold War, containment, deterrence, and American credibility. He selectively cites James McNaughton in 1966 as saying that the United States was staying in Vietnam for reasons of "credibility," but he completely ignores the first part of the quotation in which McNaughton says that the "original" reasons for the United States' involvement were "varied," and also ignores parts of the very same memo in which McNaughton contends that there were in fact many alternatives to continuing the war (1975, 48).

Careful, methodical selection of historical incidents or documents can load almost any argument. Schell's interest was in presenting a case and therefore he selectively chose his documents. It must be realized that when dealing with this type of historical evidence, the same document might be open to differing interpretations, in which case one may end up with radically different conclusions. This limitation has been considered in presenting the following decision-making models.

The models considered here are well known, for they encompass much of popular and academic debate over the United States' involvement in Vietnam as well as a growing body of literature in the study of foreign policy decision making. The labels will differ from study to study but they fall into two general categories: the "rational, goals-end" model and the "quagmire," "quicksand," or "incremental" model. Later we will divide the latter model but will keep it united for the moment for analysis specifically of the Vietnam case.

The first model paints the following picture: decision makers proceed through a series of calculated, rational, and comprehensive steps before arriving at a final decision. Clarification of goals or objectives comes first. The means thought best to achieve these goals are then decided upon, but only after a thorough search of all possible alternatives, in which all important factors are taken into account. Although variations on this theme exist, the crucial element is that decisions do not occur haphazardly; they occur for reasons. In other words, as Graham Allison's "Rational Policy Model" suggests, big things happen for big reasons; the United States simply does not "stumble into" something like Vietnam. A ten-year war constitutes a "big thing," and there must have been a "big reason" for it (Allison, 1971). The term "rational" does not imply that the decisions made are necessarily correct, but merely that they result from an orderly, disciplined process, in which clearly marked procedures lead to a final decision viewed as the best one for the situation.

Many who use or infer such a model may not specifically subscribe to each of the above elements. However, by contending that big events, such as Vietnam, do not simply occur, they intimate that somewhere along the line people went through some kind of calculated, rationalized process of decision making encompassing some or all of the above points, culminating in large-scale decisions. This model suggests that Vietnam was important, that although "previous escalation (may have) made further involvement more unavoidable . . . *judgements of and reasons for Vietnam's* 'vitalness' set the course" (Gelb 1970, 2, emphasis added). In other words, this argument assumes a commitment to long-term goals that moves decision makers toward the specific types of decisions they make.

The alternative model offers a different view of decision making, namely, that no one at any one point necessarily makes a big decision—in this case, to become involved in Vietnam. It has been referred to already as the quagmire-quicksand-incremental model, but it also bears strong resemblance to Lindblom's "Successive Limited Comparison" model (1959, 81) as well as to Graham Allison's "organizational" and "bureaucratic" models (1971). According to this alternative, successive decisions in Vietnam were not necessarily made to implement long-range goals, but for other reasons: there was nothing else to do, and it was better and easier to continue a little longer rather than back down; and decision makers felt they could not simply do nothing. Another component of this model is that organizations and bureaucracies involved in a situation each have their own respective goals that may not necessarily be synonymous with the large-scale national goals and do not necessarily relate, except in the most indirect way, to any large national interest.

Arthur Schlesinger at one time proposed the use of the quicksand metaphor for Vietnam. According to the Kennedy aide, "the policy of 'one more step' lured the United States deeper and deeper into the morass. In retrospect, Vietnam is a triumph of the politics of inadvertence. We have achieved our present entanglement, not after due and deliberate consideration, but through a series of small decisions" (cited in Ellsberg 1972, 50). Although Schlesinger later partially repudiated his description of United States Vietnam policy, Daniel Ellsberg, in using that early description, contends that it is, insofar as it applies to Vietnam, "marred by being totally wrong for each one of those decisions over the last twenty years" (1972, 50-51). In this contention Ellsberg adds two elements to the model. To be an accurate description, a quagmire model must show (1) that decisions have been made in an optimistic mood, with the general feeling that the alternative chosen is a good one, and (2) that the alternative is perceived as capable of ending the problem "for good." Ellsberg argues very persuasively against the quagmire model for Vietnam. Since decision makers were pessimistic at each point of new commitments in Vietnam, he contends, the decisions could not have resulted from successive assessments that these decisions were good and would finally solve the problem.

The quagmire, quicksand, or incremental view is quite different from a rational, goals-end perspective on Vietnam. The latter implies basically a problem-solving approach to the making of foreign policy decisions, while the former suggests more of a "satisfying" approach (Simon 1957). Encompassed within the former are bureaucratic and organizational factors. To ignore bureaucracies and the organizations and act as if the nation makes decisions in response to large-scale goals that only it faces may be painting an unrealistic picture of the decision process. Likewise, individuals, organizations, and bureaucracies (and therefore nations) may make decisions incrementally, one step at a time, often failing to see that small-scale, seemingly minor decisions will impact on whether one has to make a future decision as well as what that decision might be.

In sum, alternative and competing explanations or models are available to understand the process of decision making during the major years of the Vietnam War up to the late 1960s. While this section specified only two general approaches, the "quagmire, quicksand, or incremental" model might itself be broken down into separately distinct models. That task, however, must follow the analysis of the historical evidence.

VIETNAM AS "RATIONAL" POLICY

Lindblom's "rational-comprehensive" model of decision making suggests that the first step in the orderly process of making a decision is the isolation of the goal (1959); Graham Allison's "rational policy" model views decisions as understandable because they constitute responses to a large-scale challenge involving large-scale goals (1971). This is the "one-decision" model, in which a single decision in response to large-scale goals determines all later decisions.

Historical evidence does exist to support this model in the Vietnam case. Some analysts see early decisions setting the path in Vietnam, suggesting that the majority, if not all, of the subsequent decisions flowed from these early ones. Analysts in *The Pentagon Papers*, for instance, cite the Truman administration's aid to France as "directly involving" the United States in Vietnam and setting the course of American policy in Southeast Asia (Sheehan 1971, xi). Gelb and Betts note that on his first full day in office, President Harry Truman asked the State Department for a paper on the major problems faced by the United States. The resultant memo dealt with the United Kingdom and the Soviet Union, as well as the issues of the postwar status of Eastern Europe and the settlement of the war with Germany. In the section dealing with France, it was implied that the United States should go out of its way to placate the French, treating that country "on the basis of her potential power and influence rather than on the basis of her present strength" (1979, 27-28). Implied in the memo was United States' support for the French position in Indochina.

Gelb and Betts also cite a string of National Security Council memoranda viewed as evidence of a long-term, solid commitment. In February 1950, one such memo talked of taking "all practicable measures" to prevent further Communist expansion. Southeast Asia would be in "grave hazard" if Indochina were controlled by the Communists. An NSC document (124/2) of 25 June 1952 called Indochina "of great strategic importance" and "essential to the security of the free world." Concluded Gelb and Betts, "The basic American commitment to Vietnam was set, internally and publicly. . . . the top political leadership of the executive branch never wavered from the objective of preventing a Communist takeover" (1979, 183).

On November 18, 1952, President-elect Dwight D. Eisenhower met with Secretary of State Dean Acheson to discuss the most important issues facing the incoming president. One of these included Indochina, and Acheson, after laying out the issue for Eisenhower, suggested "This is an urgent matter upon which the new administration must be prepared to act" (Gelb and Betts 1979, 28). Then a 1954 NSC paper outlined American policy in Vietnam, and "'American policy toward post-Geneva Vietnam was drawn.' The commitment for the United States to assume the burden of defending South Vietnam had been made" (1971, 15). Thus, subsequent United States-Vietnamese relations were determined, and those involved knew it.

Some evidence hints that Kennedy's original decisions in Vietnam were calculated responses to large-scale, long-range goals. Hilsman notes that although Kennedy grumbled about being "overcommitted" in Southeast Asia, he felt he could not do otherwise in Vietnam lest he disrupt "the whole balance of power and fabric of the security structure of the region, where so many countries had based their policy on continued American involvement" (1967, 420). As a result of foreign policy setbacks at the Bay of Pigs and Berlin, and the devastating meeting with Khrushchev at Vienna in the summer of 1961—at which, most observers agreed, Kennedy lost face—David Halberstam contends that, at the time, Vietnam was also seen as going Communist, something Kennedy refused to allow (1968, 23). Eugene Eidenberg cites James Reston to the effect that Kennedy's evaluation of Khrushchev's behavior at Vienna was very bleak, leading him to put 12,000 advisors into Vietnam: "If Reston's appraisal is true, it is ironical that President Kennedy made one of his first major moves in Southeast Asia less in response to a threat within that region than a reaction to America's relations with the Soviet Union" (1969, 82). Likewise, *The Pentagon Papers* analyst suggests that because of the shift toward neutralization in Laos, the Kennedy administration felt compelled to "show strength in Vietnam to reassure America's allies" (1971, 87).

Kennedy's early decisions, then—at his death 16,000 advisors were in Vietnam as opposed to less than 1,000 when he took office—might have been motivated by the long-range goals of maintaining a balance within Southeast Asia, and communicating determination to the Soviets. Further long-range prescience is implied in Tom Wicker's suggestion that Vice-President Lyndon Johnson's report to Kennedy on his trip to Southeast Asia in May 1961 was a "blueprint" for his later actions as president "including the risk of committing 'major United States forces to the area'" (1968, 202). United States policy was judged as becoming even more determined after Kennedy's assassination: Johnson, under emotional stress, did not want Vietnam to become his "loss of China." "The tragedy of Lyndon Johnson was set in motion less than 48 hours after he had become President" (1968, 205).

Decision-Making Models

Since the war was going poorly, but certainly posed no direct and immediate threat to the United States in 1963 and 1964, decisions made then can be understood as being directed by long-range goals not necessarily linked to the specifics of the conflict. Numerous analysts have concluded, moreover, that long-range, large-scale decisions were being made at the time. Tom Wicker, for instance, asserts that the so-called Tonkin Gulf Resolution had been prepared long before the alleged attack occurred (1968, 225). Others contend that while Johnson campaigned on a peace platform in 1964 against Goldwater's strongly hawkish views, his administration planned bombing and other escalatory actions against North Vietnam (Schoenbrun 1968; Draper 1967). David Halberstam even asserts that the bombing targets were placed on Johnson's desk the day after his 1964 victory (1968, 20).

Such evidence implies that decisions to escalate were carefully planned, and must have been directed by some long-range goal. Indeed, no dearth of such long-range goals has ever existed in Vietnam. Leslie Gelb posits initial and persistently "high objectives" as the driving force behind United States involvement in Vietnam; Gelb's assertion about the "importance" proves interesting in light of the evidence presented in the previous chapter: "Statements about the vital importance of Vietnam to United States national security are a matter of the yearly public record" (1970, 11). As the Cold War heated up and the fighting between France and the Vietminh intensified, "Indochina and an anti-Communist solution in Indochina became more vital to United States leaders inside and outside the government" (1970, 18).

From the State Department's claim in 1948 that the objective was "to eliminate so far as possible Communist influence in Indochina," to Lyndon Johnson's statement in 1964, "We seek an independent, non-Communist South Vietnam," long-range, large-scale goals have been consistently verbalized. Further, as one hard indicator of Vietnam's vitalness to the United States, Gelb notes the $3.5 billion in military assistance the United State gave to France from 1945 to 1951. All of this evidence suggests that the United States was committed and that the commitment occurred early, remained consistent, and directed subsequent actions in Vietnam. A rationalized process of decision making had brought about *the* decision on Vietnam early in the game, and the rest simply followed and ratified it.

Perhaps the strongest evidence against the quagmire, if not necessarily for the rational, calculating model, is Ellsberg's demonstration that each successive decision for further commitments in Vietnam was made during pessimistic periods, and as such could not have been optimistically viewed (as the quagmire model demands) as the "final decision," the "escape hatch," the alternative to solve the problem "for good" (1972). After the Taylor-Rostow mission to Saigon in early 1961, Secretary of Defense McNamara and the Joint Chiefs agreed with Taylor's proposals encompassing minimal assistance to Vietnam "but with the significant warning that much greater troop commitments were likely in the future" (Sheehan 1971, 85). The fall of the South would lead to "fairly rapid extension of Communist control or complete accommodation to Communism, in the rest of mainland Southeast Asia and in Indonesia. The chances are against, probably sharply against, preventing that fall by any measures short of the introduction of United States forces on a substantial scale" (Sheehan 1971, 148-49). The 8,000-man "floodrelief" force suggested by Taylor in late 1961 would most likely not do the job, and "we would be almost certain to get increasingly mired down in an inconclusive struggle." The only way to achieve their goals was to convince Hanoi that full United States backing was behind the Saigon regime, and, said McNamara in 1961, "I believe we can assume that the maximum United States forces required on the ground in Southeast Asia will not exceed . . . 205,000 men" (Sheehan 1971, 148-50).

At that time fewer than 1,000 American advisors were in Vietnam. The Taylor-Rostow report had recommended aid up to and including a regular task force. Ellsberg notes:

Decision-Making Models

"With the task force, the initial program was presented as adequate for the short run, but probably inadequate for the long run, requiring major additional measures. Without the vital element of the task force, for which there was no convincing substitute, the remaining measures were almost surely inadequate for both long-term and short-term aims. President Kennedy bought the program minus the task force" (1972, 59). According to *The Pentagon Papers* analysts, the issue at the time was not simply whether to send the 8,000-man main task force but "whether or not to embark on a course that, without some extraordinary good luck, would lead to combat involvement in Southeast Asia on a very substantial scale" (Sheehan 1971, 105).

In other words, the 1961 Kennedy decision did not constitute a decision promising the end. Taylor saw the Communist strategy in broad-scale terms: they wished "to gain control of Southeast Asia by means of subversion and guerilla war.... The interim Communist goal—enroute to total takeover—appears to be a neutral Southeast Asia, detached from United States protection. This strategy is well on the way to success in Vietnam" (1971, 144).

A threat of that magnitude demanded long-range decisions, and Taylor suggested the need to develop reserve strength in the military establishment "required to cover actions in Southeast Asia up to the nuclear threshold ... the call-up of additional support forces may be required" and the only circumstance that would convince the enemy is the knowledge "that the United States has prepared itself soundly to deal with aggression in Southeast Asia *at any level*" (Sheehan 1971, 178, emphasis added).

"The loss of South Vietnam to Communism," remarked Secretary of State Dean Rusk and Secretary of Defense McNamara in November 1961, "would involve the transfer of a nation of 20 million people from the free world to the Communist bloc," and the United States might be forced to put combat troops in South Vietnam and perhaps "to strike at the source of the aggression in North Vietnam." They suggested two alternatives, the first being small units primarily to aid South Vietnam, the second being large, organized units with an actual or potential direct military mission. If the latter were introduced, then "the ultimate possible extent of our military commitment in Southeast Asia must be faced. The struggle may be prolonged, and Hanoi and Peiping may overtly intervene" (Sheehan 1971, 150-51).

The 1961 "Kennedy decisions," this historical evidence suggests, can be interpreted in a fashion quite different from "quagmire" in nature: they occurred (1) as a result of large, strategic concerns, (2) with long-range goals in mind, (3) with hardheaded assessment of large ultimate costs, and (4) with no great optimism that the decisions would achieve the "end of the tunnel." Kennedy noted in his last television interview on September 12, 1963, that anything that hindered the winning of the war was "inconsistent with our policy or our objectives." He wanted the war to be won, the Communists to be contained, and the American troops to go home: "That is our policy." Hilsman later wrote that Kennedy's comments "became a policy guideline" (1967, 505-6). Michael Nacht contends that Kennedy moved deeper and deeper into Vietnam because of the containment policy established during the 1950s and its apparent success, the increased interest in counterinsurgency programs in the Kennedy administration, and finally the "success" that Kennedy and his advisors felt they had had in the Cuban Missile Crisis (Nacht, 1980). Certainly, one could argue, Soviet Premier Nikita Khrushchev's speech of January 6, 1961, two weeks before Kennedy's inauguration, calling for more wars of "national liberation," did not go unnoticed by the new and vigorous administration.

Three years later, in the Johnson administration, perceptions of options can be viewed as having remained the same. Maxwell Taylor noted in November 1964 that if the United States discovered it was playing a losing game in South Vietnam, it must then establish an adequate government, improve the counterinsurgency program, and finally persuade or force the North to stop its aid to the Vietcong. Bundy set out similar goals, but argued for more specific

Decision-Making Models

actions, including "gradual military pressures directed systematically against the DRV (Democratic Republic of Vietnam)"; and more air strikes lasting from two to six months, starting south of the 19th parallel and working up, which could ultimately lead to strikes on all military-related targets, and a blockade of North Vietnam (Sheehan 1971, 375). Less than six months later, with the commitment of forty-four battalions in the summer of 1965, *The Pentagon Papers'* analysts argue:

> The major participants in the decision knew the choices and understood the consequences . . . it was perceived as a threshold-entrance into an Asian land war. The conflict was seen to be long, with further United States deployments to follow. The choice at that time was not whether or not to negotiate, it was not whether to hold on for a while or let go—the choice was viewed as losing South Vietnam. . . . Final acceptance of the desirability of inflicting defeat on the enemy rather than merely denying him victory opened the door to an indeterminate amount of additional force (1971, 416-17).

In July 1965, George Ball dissented from the ongoing decisions in what was to turn out to be a prophetic assessment and prediction.

> The decision you face now, therefore, is crucial. Once large numbers of U.S. troops are committed to direct combat, they will begin to take heavy casualties in a war they are ill-equipped to fight in a non-cooperative if not downright hostile countryside. Once we suffer large casualties, we will have started a well-nigh irreversible process. Our involvement will be so great that we cannot—without national humiliation—stop short of achieving our complete objectives. *Of the two possibilities, I think humiliation would be more likely than the achievement of our objectives—even after we have paid terrible costs* (Sheehan 1971, 450).

Dissent concerning the future path of the war came not only from the left, but also from the right. CIA Chief John McCone warned in 1965 that "we will find ourselves mired down in combat in the jungle in a military effort that we cannot win, and from which we will have extreme difficulty in extracting ourselves" (*Pentagon Papers, NYT* ed., 441).

In November 1965, as the American troop buildup blossomed, McNamara, although agreeing with the recommendation that four hundred thousand troops be sent to Vietnam by the end of 1966, said: "We should be aware that deployments of the kind I have recommended will not guarantee success. United States killed-in-action can be expected to reach 1,000 a month, and the odds are even that we will be faced in early 1967 with a 'no decision' at an even higher level" (Sheehan 1971, 466).

Hence, even through late 1966, it appears the decision makers knowingly involved themselves in an escalating situation, with the full realization that even new heavy commitments were most likely not going to do the job. In October 1966, when, according to *The Pentagon Papers*, McNamara was becoming more and more distressed with the war, he noted in a memo to the president: "The prognosis is bad that the war can be brought to a satisfactory conclusion within the next two years. The large-unit operations probably will not do it; negotiations probably will not do it. *While we should continue to pursue both of these routes in trying for a solution in the short run, we should recognize that success from them is a mere possibility, not a probability*" (Sheehan 1971, 549). At that time, the war had been in full swing for more than eighteen months, United States troops were still being sent to Vietnam, and future decisions would escalate the conflict even further. McNamara had pointed out only the possibility of securing any kind of victory, and yet the administration continued to march on.

Not until seventeen months after McNamara's pessimistic estimate of October 1966 were decisions finally made to reverse, at least partially, the escalation of the war. With the multitude of warnings and negative assessments, the above

Decision-Making Models 65

evidence does *not* suggest, especially for the decisions in the 1960s, that the United States inadvertently and unknowingly became bogged down through a succession of small steps, thinking each would solve the problem for good or cause it, at the very least, to go away. To the contrary, it suggests that very wide-eyed accurate assessments had been made about what Vietnam was going to be.

AN ALTERNATIVE MODEL

An alternative model suggests that American involvement in Vietnam did not result from such a well-thought-out process, with long-range goals in mind. This section presents a different picture, beginning by answering a series of questions, the first being one that was raised in the previous chapter: how important was Vietnam as an issue? Was it central or peripheral? One conclusion that can be drawn from *The Pentagon Papers* is that it seemed to be an issue of constant concern, since throughout the post–World War II period one can find references to it in many internal documents. However, the evidence presented in chapter 2 did not show Vietnam to be of primary and constant concern.

As late as 1961, David Halberstam contends, "Vietnam had not seemed important.... Even in Southeast Asia, Laos seemed more important" (1971, 59). When President Kennedy was briefed in 1961, Gelb and Betts noted that "the deteriorating situation in Southeast Asia" was the first item on the agenda. Berlin, Cuba, and strategic nuclear arms followed (1979, 28). And yet it is of note that despite the alleged importance of Southeast Asia and the concentration on Laos, Gelb and Betts observe, "Eisenhower, however, did not mention Vietnam" (1979, 29). Later, in 1964, two observers contend the war was not an issue at that time. "All the evidence visible at the time, and much testimony gathered since, suggests that, in 1964, Johnson was not deeply concerned about Vietnam" (Wicker 1968, 229). Gelb and Betts note that while ultimately "Vietnam became the high drama of the Johnson administration" (1979, 96), it had not always been that way; while Vietnam had been a "nagging" question for previous presidents, it usually remained "a secondary issue in the mosaic of international and domestic politics," and it would not be until the second half of the 1960s that the war would "come to dominate all other issues" (1979, 96). The issues in 1964 centered around Goldwater and his ideology (Halbertstam 1968, 19), or the "proper controls for nuclear weapons" (Wicker 1968, 217).

Foreign aid is a hard indicator, and Gelb's citation of the $3.5 billion in military aid to France certainly suggests the importance of Vietnam. Since the United States financed 61% of France's program in Indochina in 1954, we can safely assume that portions of that aid supported the war. Other data presents a slightly different picture, however, subsequent to 1954. Agency for International Development figures, for instance, show $3.3 billion in aid to France for the 1953-61 period; since France's operations in Indochina ended in 1954, however, it is unclear how much of this aid went to Indochina throughout the period. More important, however, is the fact that Vietnam itself ranked about eleventh during the 1953-61 period in total military aid received, behind the Netherlands, Korea, Italy, Belgium, Turkey, Greece, United Kingdom, and Japan. By 1962, Vietnam had moved up just behind Turkey. The AID figures, unfortunately, may not provide for military assistance delivered under other programs. But if relatively accurate, they suggest that although Vietnam certainly received military aid from the early 1950s, during the period from 1954 to 1962 it ranked below numerous other countries (Agency for International Development, 1971).

A second point concerns the role of long-range planning. The rational, means-ends model implies at least some role for long-range planning, and assumes that it can and does exist. It also implies that decision makers set about to find the most appropriate means to achieve prescribed goals. The goals dictate the means and not the other way around. The quagmire model suggests that an interaction process exists between the goals and the means.

Decision-Making Models   67

In a November 1961 National Security Council meeting, Kennedy reportedly asked whether it was really important to save South Vietnam and Laos (Sheehan 1971, 108). After a visit to South Vietnam in December and January 1962-63, Hilsman noted no overall planning effort in South Vietnam itself, and little or no long-range thinking about the kind of country that should emerge from a possible victory, or what could be done to contribute to that longer-range goal (1967, 465). Gelb and Betts, noting that there was opposition in the executive branch from time to time, concluded: "No comprehensive and systematic examination of Vietnam's importance to the United States was ever undertaken in the executive branch. Debates revolved around how to do things better and whether they could be done, not whether they were worth doing" (1979, 190).

Although the basic objective was often referred to as "an independent non-Communist South Vietnam" (Sheehan 1971, 323), Johnson, interestingly enough, suggested to Maxwell Taylor in December 1964 that he inform the South Vietnamese the United States could not go on "unless they were able to pull themselves together" (1971, 333). Four months later, in April 1965, Taylor cabled Washington: "I badly need a clarification of our purposes and objectives. Before I can present our case to the GVN, I have to know what that case is, and why. It is not going to be easy to get ready concurrence for the large-scale introduction of foreign troops unless the need is clear and explicit" (1971, 445).

The uncertainty of exactly what long-range goals and interests were actually at stake was reflected in specific operational decisions. Wicker, citing an official who participated in the Pleiku retaliation decisions, contends the bombing was started with "no philosophy of what we were doing. . . . We ignored the difficulty of halting the natural growth of something once started, and we considered the whole thing too much in terms of immediate effect and not enough in terms of long-range problems" (1968, 261). Wicker concludes that the bombing decision was not a policy decision meant to bring about the surrender of Hanoi, for then they would have had to decide on "strategic bombing" and make other policy decisions, which they were not willing to do. Halberstam claims the decision makers "moved toward deciding, not because they really believed in bombing for there was a good deal of private hedging on what the bombing might accomplish ('This bombing bullshit,' Lyndon Johnson called it), but because there was nowhere else to go and they did not want to send troops" (1971, 64).

Henry Graff, in his recollection of interviewing Bill Moyers, notes that at no time during the Vietnam crisis did the president make an actual "peace-or-war" decision. "The step-up of the fighting after the attack on Pleiku seemed only a promising option for ending the threat to South Vietnam" (Graff 1970, 49-50). Eidenberg cites one national security advisor to the effect that no one, including the president, knew what it would take to hold in Vietnam. "The hard fact is that the government was not asking what the implications of holding in Vietnam were. Long-range planning is very difficult in the heat of the day-to-day situation" (Eidenberg 1969, 106).

Final decisions to begin the bombing took place in early February 1965. The Vietcong attack on Pleiku had brought a single United States air attack in retaliation; a few days later an attack at Quinhon brought a similar response; and on 13 February, the sustained air war, called Rolling Thunder, was begun. *The Pentagon Papers'* analysts note there was no dearth of reasons for the bombing—there were more reasons than were required—"but in the end the decision to go ahead with the strike seems to have resulted as much from the lack of alternative proposals as from any compelling logic in their favor" (Sheehan 1971, 344).

As the war continued with no end in sight, and Secretary of Defense McNamara became more and more disenchanted, the increasingly unproductive means were taking their toll on the long-range goals. In May 1967, McNamara asked the president to eliminate the ambiguities from the objectives in Vietnam, and suggested the United States' commitment be defined to include (1) that the South Vietnamese people

Decision-Making Models

be able to determine their own future, and (2) that the United States' commitment cease if South Vietnam ceased to help itself. Further, he said, the commitment should *not* be to ensure one group's continuation in power in South Vietnam, nor that the government remain anti-Communist, nor that South Vietnam remain separate from North Vietnam (Sheehan 1971, 514). This represented a serious break from National Security Action Memorandum (NASM) 288, which had seen the goal as "an independent non-Comunist South Vietnam" (1971, 536). Recognition of this is found in the Joint Chiefs of Staff's reply on May 31, saying that McNamara's changes "would undermine and no longer provide a complete rationale for our presence in South Vietnam or much of our efforts over the past two years" (1971, 538). In other words, the strategic, large-scale goal was being changed, primarily as a result of nonproductive means.

The same interaction occurred over the decisions of early 1968 drastically reversing the war. The *New York Times* reports *"No one . . . advocated lowering objectives.* It was a time, however, when many pressures for a change of course were converging on the White House" (1969, 14, emphasis added). The pressures included the recent Tet offensive, which had punctured many notions about how the war was going; the military resources that were becoming thinner; and the fact that there really was nothing left to send to Vietnam without large draft calls, mobilization, or sending Vietnam veterans back for a second term. As the *Times* noted, all these means for achieving the goals that "nobody advocated lowering" were "extremely unappealing." The war, and the goals, were changed, however, at least for the moment and the supposedly high principles guiding the United States' commitment in Vietnam withered away once the means became untenable.

This suggests yet a third dimension along which the quagmire model can be investigated, namely the extent of the alternatives considered. If only one alternative is proposed, negative components of that alternative, which might not have been ignored had other alternatives been suggested, can be more readily bypassed. In Vietnam, some options, such as bombing, were followed not because they were perceived in a long-range sense to be necessary for fulfilling long-range goals, but because alternatives were not available, or those that were available were distasteful. Hence, any negative aspects of bombing—such as, what do we do next—were played down.

A fourth dimension concerns means and ends. Rationalized models picture decision makers as first establishing goals and then searching for means to achieve them. The quicksand model proposes a somewhat sloppier, more incremental process. Roger Hilsman reports an incident at an NSC meeting in September 1963, where Robert Kennedy raised serious questions about what the United States was doing in Vietnam. If the goal was to resist a Communist takeover, and if that could not be achieved by any prospective South Vietnamese government, then it was time to get out. Kennedy insisted the basic question—whether a Communist takeover could be resisted by any government—had not been answered, "and he was not sure that anyone had enough information to answer it" (1967, 501). The goal, it appears from this recollection, was manipulable, if means to achieve it proved distasteful. Peter Dale Scott cites Joseph C. Goulden's book on the Tonkin affair: "Persons who watched him (Johnson) that spring concluded that he was stalling; that when suddenly brought against the hard decisions required to implement his broad policy goal, he was not so confident it was worth the effort" (Goulden, 91, cited in Scott 1970). *The Pentagon Papers* likewise picture Johnson as "pushing his Administration to plan energetically for escalation" and yet "continually hesitating to translate these plans into military action" (1971, 245).

Yet a fifth perspective is to consider the similarity between this quicksand-incremental model and the organizational or bureaucratic models proposed by Graham Allison (1971). These well-known models contend that organizations have their own goals and procedures that affect the

Decision-Making Models

types of alternatives presented to major decision makers, such as a president, but that the organization's goals may not be similar, or even related to, the supposed goal of the president or the nation. Likewise, the bureaucratic politics model holds that within all bureaucracies politics is involved in the decisions finally made, and that process may bear no relation to, or even be contrary to, the supposed large-scale goal of the nation or the president. A military memo noted, for instance, that President Johnson's July 28, 1965, announcement of new troops "necessitated an overall plan clarifying the missions and deployment of the various components." In other words, no plan had been worked out for use of these new troops, but the organization's goal might be seen as garnering as much for itself as possible. The organization could develop a plan on what to do with them after they were received, and *The Pentagon Papers'* analyst concluded that if all this were true, "MACV's plan of what to do was derived from what would be available rather than the requirement for manpower being derived from any clearly thought-out military plan" (1971, 467).

A final dimension of the quicksand model shows decisions being made in small incremental steps, and we have already seen a number of illustrations of this. With reference specifically to the relationship between incrementalism and the quicksand model, however, Ellsberg notes that Kennedy's decision to reject the task force is "in flat contradiction to Schlesinger's 'quagmire' model," for Kennedy opted for steps that "every one of his advisors described as almost surely inadequate by themselves: inadequate not only to achieve long-run success but to avoid further deterioration in the mid-term" (1972, 64).

Ellsberg implies Kennedy's decision to follow what some had predicted to be an unsuccessful course meant Kennedy knew and believed it would be unsuccessful, and furthermore, that he knew it would require further commitments. The distinguishing component of the incremental model, however, is the well-known observation that humans shy away from making big decisions; anything permitting a postponement, with the possibility of avoiding the decision in the future, is attractive. Short-run, smaller decisions provide this escape hatch. Hence, Kennedy's decision can just as easily be interpreted as an indication of his hope that Vietnam would somehow disappear, and further, of his belief that his decisions would not lead automatically to large-scale involvement. When George Ball warned him his accession to an 8,000-man force would blossom to hundreds of thousands in a few years, Kennedy reportedly replied: "George, you're crazy as hell!"

Ellsberg, although arguing against a quagmire model, clearly uses aspects of an incremental model. First, he argues, presidents acquire rather rapidly a certain level of skepticism about proposals that they are told they must adopt immediately or risk certain disaster. Rather than take the big jump, they may convert decisions into sequential ones, "buying time, awaiting information, keeping options open." Second, politicians generally may exhibit these traits: "A strong focus on the short run, a hopeful attitude toward the future, a tendency to put off painful decisions in the hope, and with some confidence, that something will turn up to make the decision either unnecessary or easier: all these are part of the typical makeup of the politician" (1972, 78).

Ellsberg's contention that the quagmire model is inaccurate, at least in these situations, is far from convincing. For, to be accurate, he says, it would imply "White House wishfulness, or general and exclusive focus upon the short run, so extreme as to seem almost psychotic" (1972, 79). Why such a focus in this case proves to be psychotic, or what evidence exists that Kennedy's perceptions were similar to those of his advisors (indeed, Ellsberg is quite candid in admitting no evidence exists either way, and therefore it is anyone's guess) is left unclear.

In other words, decision makers follow certain paths "not because they *will* work, work better, cheaper, or faster, but because such a policy *might* work, and the alternatives would fail, and failure would be 'unacceptable' or 'intoler-

Decision-Making Models   73

able'" (Ellsberg 1970, 19). Such a model goes "some part of the way to restoring something like a quicksand model" (1970, 22). Indeed, it does, and Ellsberg elaborates a crucial "presidential decision rule," namely, "Do not lose South Vietnam to Communist control—or appear to do so—before the next election" (1972, 132). Although the final settlement in Vietnam was of course a result of multiple factors, nonetheless it must be noted that the Vietnam Peace Settlement did occur in January 1973, exactly two months after Nixon's landslide election over George McGovern—and during Nixon's constitutionally determined final term in office. Decision makers probably did act under such a constraint, which confirms the hypothesis that they acted for the short run, incrementally, and aimed for gains that would achieve short-term political or bureaucratic goals. To try to impose a rational, long-term, means-ends explanation on such foreign policy decisions might be to grossly misunderstand the reasons for important decisions.

Hence, it appears that United States decision makers were driven by short-term, quicksand, or incremental processes. Solutions at various turning points were "to turn away from long-run aims and the measures associated with them, concentrating almost exclusively upon the aim of minimizing the short-run risk of anti-Communist collapse or Communist takeovers" (1972, 105). Gelb's insistence that successive presidents since Truman have been conscious of what they were doing loses some of its force when he says that decision makers "seemed to hope more than believe that something would happen. They looked to what they could not count on—a military breakthrough, an unrevealed weakness by the Vietnamese Communists, a metamorphosis of our Vietnamese, a surprise and favorable negotiated settlement—to relieve them from the ultimate responsibility of deciding 'to win or get out'" (1970, 11).

While many find it almost impossible to believe that top-level decision makers in the crucial area of foreign policy actually behave this way, nonetheless, it remains a pervasive pattern of decision making. This fact can perhaps best be illustrated by recalling the contention that had President Kennedy lived and had he been re-elected in 1964 to a second term, Vietnam would not have progressed as it did; and that in fact, as we will see shortly, Kennedy was planning on pulling out during his second term. Given this, Hilsman's scenario of what might have occurred had Kennedy lived is quite revealing. Although Kennedy opposed the bombing of trails in Laos and South Vietnam, says Hilsman, nonetheless if information had shown the North stepping up the use of infiltration routes, he would have favored placing a division of American troops in Thailand as a warning, coupled with the communication to the North of the seriousness of the situation. If these actions went unheeded, the division could be moved to the Laotian border and a second division introduced into Laos. "If that set of warnings was also ignored, a division would be introduced into Vietnam, and so on—not to fight the Viet Cong, which should remain the task of the South Vietnamese, but to deter the North from escalating" (1968, 533-34). While at the same time arguing that Kennedy would not have turned the war into an American one, he notes that if the North continued infiltration, Kennedy might have used American ground forces, but "would not have ordered them to take over the war effort from the Vietnamese, but would have limited their mission to that of occupying ports, airfields, and military bases to demonstrate to the North Vietnamese that they could not win the struggle by a policy of escalation either" (1968, 536-37).

This scenario describes perfectly the incremental process. Ellsberg is correct in saying each decision may not have been viewed as the "final" one, but they certainly were viewed as plausible options for communicating serious intent—supposedly forcing the enemy to back down. None of these decisions did bring enemy capitulation or retreat, but simply added to the burgeoning United States commitment.

The Pentagon Papers' analysts seem to agree; the Kennedy decision to build up combat support and advisory missions was made "almost by default" because the administra-

Decision-Making Models

tion was "focused so heavily in the fall of 1961 on the question of sending ground combat units to Vietnam. That decision was reached 'without extended study or debate' or precise expectations of what it would achieve" (1971, 113). Later, in the Johnson administration, a picture emerges of a president who was on the one hand "pushing his administration to plan energetically for escalation" and "continually hesitating to translate these plans into military action" (1971, 245).

The quagmire-incremental model describes decisions right to the end of the American escalation. In the spring of 1967, General William Westmoreland asked for 200,000 more troops, but admitted that if the request were granted, the Vietcong would also likely add more troops, and that, potentially, the war could last for five more years. McNaughton wrote in a memo to McNamara in May that the option of limiting the request to an 80,000-man "add-on" force would only postpone the serious decision of a reserve call-up, "but postpone is all that it does—probably to a worse time, 1968. Providing the 80,000 troops is tantamount to acceding the whole Westmoreland-Sharp request. This being the case, they will 'accept' the 80,000. But six months from now, in will come the messages like the '470,000-570,000' messages, saying that the requirements remain at 201,000 or more" (1971, 534).

This is more or less what happened. When General Westmoreland requested 206,000 more troops in early 1968, after the Tet offensive, none of those called together by Secretary of Defense Clark Clifford to evaluate the request favored it totally, yet none favored turning it down. "Several insiders later suggested that a smaller request, for 30,000 to 50,000 men, would probably have been granted and the Administration's crisis would have been avoided or at least delayed" (*New York Times*, 1969). All-out involvement was avoided because of domestic and other concerns; and complete pullout was also rejected because of political unpleasantries and disinclination to make the big decision reversing everything that had already been done.

The foregoing evidence enables us to be reasonably secure in concluding that Vietnam was not a central issue early on to foreign policy makers. Furthermore, decisions concerning Vietnam consisted of small incremental steps, each of which, it was only hoped, would make the problem go away. Specific decisions (such as sending ground troops or starting a bombing program), were not made necessarily because they would achieve the long-range goal or large-scale strategy, but because (1) they *might* do that, (2) alternatives were not considered, or (3) alternatives were too distasteful. Because of this, thorough analyses of alternatives and their possible results were often not made. In the final analysis, distasteful means often affected the choice of goals. The end result is a picture of incremental decisions, a decision-making process far from comprehensive or rationally calculated, and long-range goals far from the guiding light leading to successive decisions.

EVALUATION OF COMPETING MODELS

A few introductory comments should be made before presenting an evaluation of these competing models. First, these are not strictly delineated and tightly defined models, but rather perspectives on decision making. Second, the categorization of any individual analyst or scholar into either one of the models does not necessarily mean that that individual agrees with every component of the model. Third, it should be clear by now that each model suggests different "lessons" about Vietnam, and puts the decision makers of the time in quite contrasting perspectives. Finally, it should also be clear that these models of decision-making are loose in the sense that the factors we are investigating are evaluated by using historical evidence which in most instances cannot be quantified, and therefore is conducive to a much more subjective evaluation. However, it is helpful to at least make a stab at suggesting ways of evaluating these models rather than simply adhering to one or the other or saying that "they both explain Vietnam."

One technique for evaluating the models is to examine

the assumptions on which the models rest. A rational perspective assumes Vietnam could not have just happened; smaller events, perhaps, yes, but not something as momentous as a ten-year war resulting in over fifty thousand American deaths. Ellsberg asserts that regardless of ideological positions on the war, one can only come away from a survey of internal evidence with the question: "How could they?" How could the four presidents involved "in the face of intelligence estimates and program analyses and recommendations like these, so persistently choose programs that were presented at the time of decision as almost surely inadequate in the long run, while potentially costly and risky, instead of measures purported to be either more effective or else requiring lesser involvement?" (1972, 74).

The underlying implication appears to be that the decision makers must have had big reasons for doing what they did, and we should not propose to understand such large events by citing reasons for not doing what they did not do, namely, pull out of Vietnam altogether. But looked at from the 1980s the Vietnam War does not look the same as when looked at from the early and mid-1960s. Pessimism and optimism were both present while decisions were being made; perhaps, when optimism reigned, the probability that Vietnam would become a prolonged, deadly, and indecisive war seemed very small.

A second assumption is that authentic reasons for presidential actions can be found in presidential statements. If accurate, this undermines the quicksand model, for verbalized long-range goals abound throughout the Vietnam conflict, and the record is clear that decision makers often referred to Vietnam as "vital." In addition, perusing the *Pentagon Papers*, one is struck by what appears to be constant and consistent concern over Vietnam throughout the post-World War II period. The previous chapter showed that important symbols thought to describe and justify our involvement in Vietnam were present throughout the 1961-72 period.

On investigation, however, this assumption is questionable. First, using the *Pentagon Papers* as a reflection of constant, high concern toward Vietnam is misleading. Any set of documents devoted solely to one issue is certain to give that impression; it is a carefully drawn (and biased) sample of decision maker "concern." Although one can find statements of decision-maker "concern" over Vietnam for every year in the post-World War II period (Chapter 2), nonetheless the evidence suggests that those years of high and intense concern over Vietnam were in the minority, and were, in fact, primarily the years in which major involvement was occurring—the times when we would expect decision maker concern to be high.

Some might argue, however, that greater attention will be devoted to an area—of necessity—once large-scale war breaks out, and that this increased attention, which does show up in every one of these measures, does not prove the situation was unimportant before that time. Although certainly a valid rejoinder to simple quantitative indicators, nonetheless the burden of proof remains on those arguing that Vietnam had always been vital and important. The fact that each president may have referred to Vietnam as "vital" at one point or another does not necessarily signify constant and high concern, nor do these scattered references to Vietnam annually mean the "path had been set," or, more important, that in the decision-makers' minds, such "vitalness" would lead to all-out, full-scale war.

The problem is whether we can believe such public pronouncements. Ellsberg relates an incident that occurred in the spring of 1963. Senator Mike Mansfield had been arguing that increasing American troop involvement in Vietnam was a mistake. President Kennedy told Mansfield he agreed with his arguments, but that he was helpless to do anything before the 1964 election, lest a conservative backlash erupt against the president for having "pulled out." Ellsberg quotes Presidential Assistant Kenneth O'Donnell on the incident.

> After Mansfield left the office, the President told me that he had made up his mind that after his re-election he would take the risk of unpopularity and make a complete

withdrawal of American forces from Vietnam. "In 1965, I'll be damned everywhere as a Communist appeaser. But I don't care. If I tried to pull out completely now, we would have another Joe McCarthy red scare on our hands, but I can do it after I'm re-elected. So we had better make damned sure that I *am* re-elected" (Ellsberg 1972, 97).

Two points deserve note here. First, if we can believe this account as an accurate reflection of Kennedy's true perceptions—and Ellsberg does—then it hardly fits the stereotype of the president perceiving Vietnam as vital enough to stay, regardless of future consequences. But more important, especially since Gelb's argument rests on four successive presidents having publicly called Vietnam "vital," is Ellsberg's remark, in the original version of his quagmire paper, that "the fact that the President continued to make contradictory *public statements* of the sort he did is of *no* weight in opposing this account" (1970, 40; first emphasis added). Thus, regardless of Kennedy's public posture, which included labeling Vietnam "vital," Ellsberg concludes that he was clearly interested in cutting bait. This calls into question the reliability of at least some official, public pronouncements about the vitalness of Vietnam. Gelb and Betts in essence agree.

In part what they were saying about Vietnam until 1965 was nothing more than the typical rhetoric used to justify security aid programs. Official rhetoric, classified and public, was not known for its discriminating qualities. "Vitals" and "great importances" cluttered the run of speeches and documents, especially after Acheson's perimeter speech, in which he failed to indulge in such clutter, was often blamed for the Korean War. Using words for the purposes of deterrence, bolstering allies, and appeasing the domestic audience was routine (1979, 191).

Furthermore, without information on whether those involved used such words as "vital" or "commitment" in reference to other countries or areas, evaluating their use of these terms with reference to Vietnam is difficult. Decision makers have public verbal profiles, and quite possibly they use such words in a variety of situations, in which case they constitute little more than verbal baggage. Hence, appearance of such words may not necessarily imply long-term interest and high-level involvement and commitment.

Another method of evaluation is the analysis of inferences required from the models. The clear inferences required from the quagmire model as first outlined by Schlesinger are that (1) decision makers are optimistic at important decision points, and (2) new commitments are perceived as promising to do the job for good. Ellsberg questions both of these inferences, especially for the 1961 Kennedy decisions.

In terms of the first inference, Ellsberg's data (along with other evidence from *The Pentagon Papers* presented earlier) are quite clear in showing that decisions in 1961 to aid Vietnam short of the task force were not results of optimism that this would do it. Without the task force, said Maxwell Taylor, the United States' program in South Vietnam could not succeed. While clearly not hedging, however, other elements surrounding the decision should be noted. First, Taylor was a military man, and might be expected to opt for a military solution. While certainly not true in all instances, it would probably be safe to conclude that military advisors would normally tend to opt more often for military solutions, and civilian advisors to opt for civilian solutions.

Second, although the introduction of the task force would offer more advantages than risks, Taylor also noted the risks: sending the task force would further weaken the strategic United States reserve force; United States prestige would become more engaged; and "if the first contingent is not enough to accomplish the necessary results, it will be difficult to resist the pressure to reinforce" (Sheehan 1971, 141). The alternatives Kennedy faced, then, were: (1) he could send aid short of the task force (the decision he ultimately opted for); (2) he could commit the 8,000-man task force, and run risks of escalation; or (3) he could pull out. But there was both optimism and pessimism about all three

Decision-Making Models

alternatives. Although pessimism certainly surrounded the alternative Kennedy did choose, it also applied to the full-scale task force; and certainly, given bureaucratic dislike of reversing fields, a complete pullout had much more going against it. At this point decision makers were not optimistically striding into Vietnam; all of the options carried pessimistic as well as optimistic views. That some options were seen as less pessimistic than others does not mean they were viewed optimistically. In terms of later decisions, Irving Janis concludes:

> As for the alleged "pessimism of later 1964," the available evidence does not show an impressive degree of fit with Ellsberg's hypothesis that the President and his advisors had a realistic view of what their escalation decisions would accomplish. When we look at *The Pentagon Papers*, we find that the conferees sometimes did talk about the possibility that the war might last for years, but we also find a number of direct contradictions of Ellsberg's statement that unrealistic hopes were not a prominent factor in the major escalation decisions of late 1964 and early 1965 (1972, 108-9).

Further, while Ellsberg demonstrates that decision makers seldom saw any of their alternatives as doing the job for good, none of that evidence precludes the possibility of an incremental model of decision making. Perhaps the requirements for the quagmire model, as set out by Ellsberg, are simply too strict. The answer to the question, "How could they do it?" with all the pessimism concerning the alternatives, is to be found in much of Ellsberg's analysis: they thought their decisions *might* work, at least getting them off the hook until the next decision. As noted already, the cleanest distinction can be made between the rational policy or goals-ends model, on the one hand, and a conglomerate including the bureaucratic-organizational-quicksand-quagmire-incremental components on the other. However, it might be helpful to distinguish between the quicksand and incremental models.

For the quicksand model as outlined by Ellsberg to be accurate, two elements must be present: decision makers first must be optimistic about their decisions, and second must perceive them as solving their problem "for good." Ellsberg thinks this model is not appropriate, at least for what he calls the "crucial" decision points throughout the Vietnam War. The reason is that although optimism was present, it occurred only after decisions had been made. Further, none of the chosen alternatives were looked upon as solving their problem "for good." Ellsberg establishes fairly rigid criteria.

For an incremental model to be accurate, however, decision makers need only view their decisions as possible solutions; each decision is taken one at a time, and no great attention is focused on long-range concerns. It correlates with a presidential decision-making pattern described by Richard Moorsteen. Presidents learn to question arguments that they must act immediately or face dire consequences; they often convert decisions into small, sequential ones rather than large-scale ones; they may not reject an alternative outright lest they dash someone's hopes; they develop, as politicians, short-run perspectives with the belief that, usually, things work themselves out "in the long run" (Ellsberg, 1972). In sum, there is a strong drive to "do something," and often no clear idea exists of what exactly the decision is supposed to accomplish. All of these elements combine to produce small, seemingly minor decisions.

But in a practical application of choosing one model over the other, to think that because advisors were pessimistic, the person ultimately making the decision was also pessimistic may not be correct. In doing that, we ignore the existence of the decision itself; if we infer that the decision to go ahead—even if only partially—represents a type of optimism, then an incremental model is to that degree supported. Leaders involved in any foreign policy problem are constantly torn between optimism and pessimism, and the decisions, especially if they constitute, as in Vietnam, less than all-out decisions to plow forward, reflect this duality. By focusing on only one part of the evidence—namely the

Decision-Making Models

decision itself, which suggests at least partial optimism—a crucial piece of evidence supporting an incremental model is bypassed.

The obvious thrust of the foregoing argument is that both models—goals-means and incremental—are applicable, but at different levels and with regard to different decisions. That is, large-scale goals and objectives (such as "containing communism") provide the generalized framework within which the Vietnam War can be understood. Because of these goals, the United States decided to stay. But more tactical, immediate decisions resulted from an incremental process. No doubt historians in evaluating the large sweeps of the cold war will interpret the Vietnam War in just this way.

It does not, however, accord entirely with the data presented here, for enough evidence shows that the so-called large-scale concerns were not so large after all: Johnson's 1964 request of the CIA for an assessment of how important South Vietnam was; the JCS noting in 1954 that Indochina was not militarily important; Kennedy's plans to get out of Vietnam after his re-election, among many others. Despite the many verbalized goals we can find intimating large-scale concerns, enough contradictory evidence can be cited to gnaw away at that argument.

Such an intermingling of the two perspectives, however, does not allow for relationships and interactions between the two levels, for it assumes a neat separation between large-scale and small-scale decisions. Small decisions can become tyrannous, and few have the ability—as George Ball did—to relate each of these innocuous decisions to their potentially large-scale effect, once added to other equally innocuous looking decisions. Ellsberg solves this problem by analytically isolating the large from the small decisions. For him, decisions in 1950 to aid the French, to further support Diem in 1954, to increase the advisors in 1960, and start the bombing in 1964 are the crucial qualitative decision points. Other decisions, such as Kennedy's to increase the number of advisors, or Johnson's increase in troop commitment after 1965, are "merely quantitative" for Ellsberg (1972:51).

However, none of these large decisions occurred in a vacuum. Kennedy's decision to send Maxwell Taylor to Vietnam in the first place may have been prompted by reasons unrelated to saving Vietnam. Once the mission occurred, however, and recommendations were made, then the situation was transformed: a further decision had to be made on the recommendations. Likewise, indications are that some of Johnson's early bombing decisions were little more than feelers to see what would happen. Although certainly cloaked in broader concerns, and although perhaps considered in earlier contingency planning, evidence suggests that they were partially seen only as promising responses for the moment. The difficulty, of course, is that each promising response thereby changes the existing situation.

In other words, isolating the large-scale decisions may fail to show the effect earlier decisions had on them. Even Ellsberg argued in the first version of his quagmire paper that a quicksand model does have utility in explaining some decisions in Vietnam, but not the "first, knowing step" into the bog. The very attraction of an incremental perspective, however, is the realization that such "steps" may not exist; to act as if large decisions occur unrelated to what went before them is empirically incorrect. The incremental model requires no such large decisions.

These findings do not make the incremental model the only accurate description of Vietnam decisions, but they certainly suggest it as a very effective competitor to the rational, calculated, goals-means model. Although analyses such as those by Ellsberg and Gelb are primarily critiques of the quagmire model and do not necessarily try to support the goals-means model, they tend to move toward that end of the spectrum when they say the presidents became involved "with their eyes open, knowing why.... The deepening involvement was not inadvertent, but mainly deductive. It flowed with sureness from the perceived stakes and attendant high objectives" (Gelb and Betts 1979, 240). We say the same thing when we contend that a hypothetical observer throughout the cold war, viewing certain presiden-

Decision-Making Models

tial motives ("not losing Vietnam *this* year") and with information about how both the South and the North would perform, could then "have calculated during most of that fifteen-year period that there was a high probability that large numbers of U.S. troops would end up fighting in Vietnam, with U.S. planes bombing throughout Indochina. He would have predicted that they would be sent if necessary to avoid defeat, and that they would be necessary" (Ellsberg 1972, 123). The implication is clearly that even if decision makers did not necessarily know the effect of their decision in terms of the specific lives and costs it would incur, they chose knowing "at the moment of their escalating decisions that new crises or challenges to larger efforts would probably return" (1972, 125).

Hence, the calculating, goals-means model as applied to the Vietnam case might have some validity as well as some suggestive evidence. At the same time, it has some serious drawbacks as the sole interpreter of the American involvement in Vietnam. Because some decision makers were able to predict what might happen with each accession of troops in Vietnam (such as George Ball's warning to Kennedy) this by no means is evidence that everyone agreed such an eventual outcome was likely and yet plowed ahead nonetheless.

Evidence suggests strongly that decision makers may not have, or may not exercise, the facility for long-range forecasting and planning as rationalized models require. Among the lessons we can learn from Vietnam are the following: that much decision making is incremental and sloppy, that the normal human inability and reluctance to foresee long-run consequences as well as take decisive action occurs as much in foreign affairs as in individual affairs, and that disastrous events are as likely to result from this human frailty as from human calculation.

CONCLUSION

The goal of this chapter has been to look at the process of decision making relevant to the American involvement in the Vietnam War from two different perspectives or models of decision making. It is not meant to blame or berate but simply to assess. In the wake of the war, decision makers are being judged. Certainly one's judgment should be informed by as broad a perspective on the Vietnam involvement as possible, and a broad perspective does not come from imposing one rigid model of decision making. The opposite side of the coin, however, is that just as no one should be in the business of absolving anyone of his errors in judgment, it is unseemly to look for scapegoats when errors are committed—a phenomenon that went on after the State Department allegedly "lost" China in 1949. It is to be hoped that the same phenomenon will not occur over Vietnam.

4. Moods and Public Opinion: Background for Decisions

This chapter broadens the scope of our investigation of decision making by looking at larger dynamic processes that serve as background factors within which the decision process takes place. In the case of Vietnam it is the frame within which the various perceptions of Vietnam and the definition of the Vietnam situation emerged. It is a truism that individuals make decisions and they are ultimately responsible for them; still we cannot disregard the fact that decision makers do not operate in vacuums.

We have isolated two closely related background characteristics that are often viewed as important factors in the making of foreign policy. The first is mood, elusive and hard to pinpoint, but characterized by the fluctuating way the American public and leaders view the role of the United States in the world. Moods may serve as either background restraints or license in conducting foreign policy; and they are related to changes in the conduct of American foreign policy over time. The second background characteristic is public opinion, in our case concerning the Vietnam War and American foreign policy. While public opinion will be analyzed separately, it will also be seen as partly confirming the mood notion.

These large-scale background factors do not cause specific decisions or phenomena such as the Vietnam War as opposed to some other phenomenon (rapprochement between the United States and China), or other wars (such as a war in

Laos or a war between Iraq and Iran). Thus background factors cannot necessarily help us understand the Vietnam War in a strictly causal sense; they are not point specific, which means they cannot predict to a specific event, decision, or phenomenon. An analogy might be what economists call the "business cycle," which simply means that there are business boom periods followed by recessions or depressions, followed once again by a business boom and so on. Despite the contention by some in the late 1960s that such cycles were a thing of the past and that economists had finally managed to get such a handle on the economy that they could fine-tune that beast and therefore such cycles were outmoded, they seem to persist with some tenacity nonetheless (Klein 1976).

We also know what tends to happen within boom and bust periods; in boom periods, there are likely to be a larger proportion of business success stories, while in bust periods more companies are likely to fail. It was not necessarily the bust period that caused Mother Fletcher's Screen Door Company to go belly up, nor the boom period that caused it to expand into the widget business, for both of those phenomena might have occurred anyway. Moreover, there are business failures in boom times and business successes in recessionary times. But the point is that the boom and the bust periods provide the background factors that enable companies to more easily fail or succeed, even though the specific and direct causal linkage for that success or failure may be something unrelated to the broader historical context.

Just as these characteristics are helpful in understanding economic point specific phenomena, such as a specific business success or failure, so also background characteristics in the field of international politics provide broader perspectives on such point specific phenomena as the Vietnam War. Once again, these background characteristics did not cause the war just as we could not say that a bust period in the economy caused the failure of Mother Fletcher's company. But just as Mother Fletcher might want to go beyond internal speculation (Was it that extra ten thousand widgets that

Moods and Public Opinion

we ordered at five dollars each that did us in?) and realize that the decision had been made in a certain external business period, likewise we might profit from knowing in what period of United States' foreign policy the Vietnam decisions were made.

Many observers are rightly dubious concerning the importance and effect of such broadly defined phenomena as moods, and may see them as being too deterministic. One of the goals of this work, however, is to illustrate the possibility of investigating questions about United States foreign policy by means of systematic, quantitative evidence. The data in this chapter perhaps highlight more than any other in this book how this goal might be achieved. If decisions are not made in a vacuum, what empirical evidence can be used to analyze the background factors that have a bearing on foreign policy decisions?

AMERICAN FOREIGN POLICY MOODS

Frank Klingberg is one of many who have suggested the notion that American foreign policy exhibits alternating moods. While these moods cannot be set out as strictly causal variables directly affecting any specific American foreign policy actions, they nonetheless serve as background factors setting the stage for certain types of policies to be formulated or disregarded (1952).

Klingberg called the moods "introversion" and "extroversion." An introvert mood is one in which the nation is either uninvolved in foreign relations or in which those relations are of a very low intensity and limited in scope. An extrovert mood, on the other hand, is one in which the nation is heavily involved in world affairs across a broad scope of activities and with great intensity. Two other terms that have commonly been used to describe the same phenomena are "isolationist" and "interventionist," the first analogous to an introvert phase and the second to an extrovert phase. These latter terms are less desirable, however, because they have different implications. Extroversion in foreign affairs does not always equate with military or religious crusading, and introversion does not necessarily equate with isolationism. Rather, the moods are relative. One introvert phase could consist of rather rigidly defined isolationism, while another introvert phase might mean that relative to the extrovert phase that preceded it, the foreign activity of the nation was reduced in scope and intensity. Likewise, some extrovert phases could consist of extensive foreign military involvement including war, while another might only mean more foreign involvement compared to the previous introvert phase. An important component of this notion of moods, of course, is that they alternate from one to the other, with an introvert phase following upon, and reacting to, an extrovert phase, and once having run its course, giving way to yet another extrovert phase.

To investigate his hunches, Klingberg generated a number of empirical indicators to measure the activity of United States foreign policy along this introvert-extrovert dimension. His findings are quite interesting. In what he calls a "rapid survey of American foreign relations," he paints a general picture of the alternation between the two types of moods. "The acts or utterances of the Government are regarded as the basic indices—events such as treaties, wars, armed expeditions, annexations, diplomatic warnings, Presidential messages and the like" (1952, 241). He found four introvert and four extrovert phases based on his general picture (table 3). Klingberg also used several statistical series, including annual naval expenditures. Although these normally increase at all times, he asserts that "a significant difference between introvert and extrovert phases may be present in the relative *rate* of increase, which is considerably greater during the extrovert phases" (1952, 257).

In a later analysis, Michael Roskin argued that Pearl Harbor constituted one paradigm calling for interventionism, and was followed by another one, Vietnam, which called for limitationism (1974). Roskin's intuitive assessment parallels Klingberg's. Roskin's analysis is not as long, covering only 1870 to 1970, but he notes four different peri-

Table 3. Introvert and Extrovert
Phases in U.S. Foreign Policy

Introvert Dates	Extrovert Dates
1776 - 1798	1798 - 1824
1824 - 1844	1844 - 1871
1871 - 1891	1891 - 1919
1919 - 1940	1940 -

SOURCE: Klingberg (1952, 250), table 1.

ods during that time. The first was the continental period, the 1870s-1880s, in which there were virtually no American troops abroad; Congress was obstructive; and there were no funds for overseas development. The imperial period, the 1890s to the 1910s, was a period when troops were in many areas of the world, Congress was cooperative with the president, and there were war loans outstanding. The Versailles period, lasting into the late 1930s, showed only few troops abroad (mainly in the Caribbean and the Philippines), Congress was again obstructive, and there was a begrudging of war debts. The Pearl Harbor period, 1940s-60s, showed American troops in Europe, Asia, Latin America, and Africa; Congress was by and large cooperative; and the United States had started the Marshall Plan and Point Four aid programs. These shifts are more or less in line with Klingberg's and the time periods are fairly closely aligned. Hence, the contention that American foreign policy does swing back and forth between introverted and extroverted eras does receive a substantial amount of support.

We now turn to analysis of Klingberg's evidence on presidential messages. We do so for several reasons. First, it bears strong resemblance to that presented earlier on attention to Vietnam and the fluctuation in presidential use of symbolic rhetoric. Second, it is readily available and quite simple to generate, and yet, despite some problems with such data, a strong case can be made for its face validity. Third, it is for the most part unobtrusive, which means that decision makers cannot contaminate the evidence in order

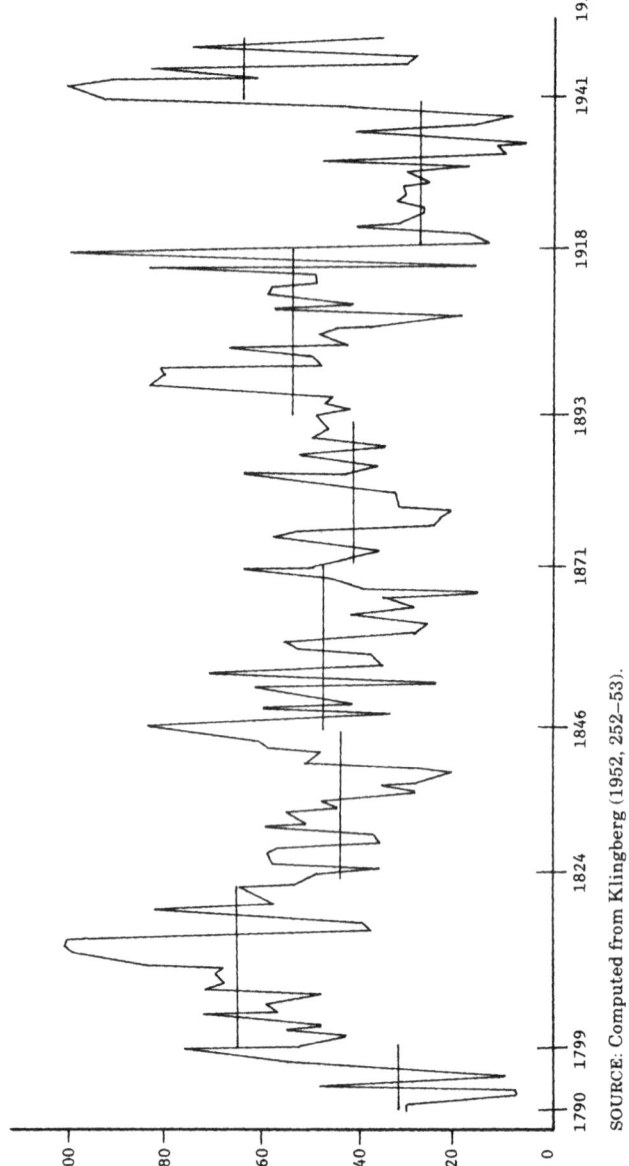

Figure 8. Percentage of the State of the Union Address Devoted to Foreign Affairs, 1790–1950

SOURCE: Computed from Klingberg (1952, 252–53).

Moods and Public Opinion 93

to mislead (unlike the post-facto interview approach). This evidence is frequently generated years, decades, and even centuries before the social scientist interested in moods came along and thought about studying it in the way to be proposed. This does not mean that decision makers do not try to mislead, but as should become clear it is virtually impossible in the present case. Thus, in generating evidence other than the statistical data we have looked at so far, Klingberg operated under the same assumption we have used, namely that investigation of the verbal output of presidents can aid in answering questions concerning possible patterns in American foreign policy.

Using State of the Union messages, Klingberg developed three different measures to assess foreign policy moods and to see if the introvert-extrovert time phases would be confirmed. He looked at the percentage of each message devoted to (1) foreign policy in general, (2) descriptions of or demands for positive action abroad, and (3) the importance of foreign affairs to the United States.

Of these three measures, Klingberg relied most for his conclusions on the second measure, namely the number of descriptions of or demands for positive action abroad. He found remarkable periodicity in this measure, with the extrovert periods (calls for action abroad) lasting roughly 27 years (ranging from 26 to 28 years), and the introvert periods (fewer calls for foreign action) averaging about 21 years (ranging from 20 to 22 years). This measure of Klingberg's corresponds the closest to the fluctuation in his statistical evidence presented earlier, thus suggesting some agreement between two very different types of indicators.

If we investigate the more general indicator, however, namely the percentage of the State of the Union messages devoted to foreign affairs, the periodicity does not show up as clearly, yet high and low attention to foreign affairs can be detected and these variations tend to correspond with Klingberg's periods (figure 8). The greatest difference between the two measures occurs in the third introvert period; where Klingberg's more judgmental measure shows it starting in 1871, these data suggest it probably began about 1864, a seven-year difference. Four other cases were off by one year, and two other cases had, respectively, three and four years' difference. Thus, with the more general measure, the introvert periods roughly are 20, 20, 37, and 20 years, for an average of 24 years as compared to Klingberg's 21. The first three extrovert periods are about 25, 17, and 22, for a mean of 21, compared to 27 years for Klingberg. However, if we include the last introvert period, begun, according to Klingberg in 1941 and argue that it ended in 1968—a point we come to momentarily—then the extrovert periods average 23 years in length to Klingberg's 27. The War of 1812, the Mexican War, the Civil War, the Spanish-American War, World War I, and World War II all fell into extrovert periods according to Klingberg's more sensitive measure. The only difference that occurred with the broader measure concerned the Civil War, which fell into an introvert period.

Hence, the general measure does detect some rather clear alternating levels—on the average—across the 1790 to 1950 period. This pattern is highlighted in the last three periods, beginning about 1900. With one exception that first period normally has well over 40% devoted to foreign affairs. The following period, after the end of World War I and encompassing the interwar era, shows only one year above 40%. Again, during the following period, up to 1950, there are fluctuations above and below 50%, with a rough average, however, of about 55%-60%.

In order to assess changing moods it would not be inaccurate, therefore, to utilize the third measure, namely the amount devoted to foreign affairs as a percentage of the total length of the State of the Union address. This measure is preferable over other measures, even though it does deviate from the more judgmental data, because it involves much less such subjective judgment. Assessing either the number of descriptions of or demands for positive action on the part of the United States abroad, or the importance of foreign relations to the United States is much more subjective than assessing the simple amount devoted to foreign affairs.

So far we have been discussing descriptions of past historical patterns. What relevance does this have to the Vietnam War? Klingberg, writing in 1952, suggested that Pearl Harbor in 1941 ushered in an extrovert period that would last into the 1960s: "All things considered—in view of America's past record, and of the presumed role of 'internal factors' in promoting the introvert-extrovert rhythm—it seems logical to expect America to retreat, to some extent at least, from so much involvement, and perhaps to do so sometime in the 1960s" (1952, 271-72).

Was Klingberg correct? An answer to that question is difficult to come by, but we will try. Extrapolating out from 1941 for twenty-seven years brings us to 1968. As of Klingberg's writing in 1952, World War II had already occurred during the extrovert phase, and the United States was then involved in the Korean War. Here the Vietnam involvement comes into the picture. As many have argued, there was early involvement in Vietnam on the part of the United States, to be sure. The United States had aided France before 1954, had considered direct involvement when Dien Bien Phu was falling that year, and by 1956, after the Geneva agreements ending direct French involvement, the United States was already rather strongly aligned (although not yet necessarily committed) to Vietnam. Around the world, furthermore, the United States became more and more committed. America gave aid to the Shah of Iran in 1953, assistance to conservative forces in Guatemala in 1954, and continued support for the South Korean government and the exiled nationalist government of Taiwan. The period was also marked by a succession of crises mostly between the United States and Russia, including the 1962 Cuban Missile Crisis, but also including several with China over the islands between the People's Republic of China and Taiwan.

All of this occurred within the confines of the cyclical period of extroversion as suggested by Klingberg. While this phase or mood of American foreign policy did not cause any of these specific events, including American involvement in Vietnam, nonetheless all of this involvement occurred against the backdrop of the most recent extroverted phase of United States foreign policy.

Official American involvement in Vietnam, in terms of actual military action, ended in January 1973, and in terms of actual American presence and aid, in April 1975, when the last remaining Americans fled in helicopters as the North Vietnamese finally conquered Saigon. A plausible argument can be made that the end of the Vietnam involvement did in fact usher in yet another introverted period. Some illustrative evidence for this contention will be presented shortly, but assuming for the moment that it is valid, then the most recent extroverted period would have been either thirty-two or thirty-four years in length, depending upon where one makes the cutting point.

However, a plausible argument can also be made that the nadir of American commitment to Vietnam in a positive and intense way occurred earlier, perhaps around 1968 to 1970. The symbolic commitment as well as the attention indicators presented in chapter 2 showed that regardless of the measure utilized, peaks occurred by about 1967-68. Likewise, using different data, Miller and Sigelman (n.d.) found that along a hawk-dove dimension, President Lyndon Johnson was becoming increasingly dovish from August 1967 to March 1968. Nineteen sixty-eight was also the year that saw the peak in both American troop strength and direct American casualties.

We know that American involvement in the war continued at a fairly intense pace, although primarily through the use of air power. But foreign policies such as the American involvement in Vietnam are not unlike large national economies or supertankers: it is frequently difficult to reverse their directions in short order. The fact that the American combat presence continued in Vietnam until late 1972 does not necessarily contradict the hypothesis that in terms of America's commitment to an extroverted policy, a reversal had actually set in prior to the final withdrawal. American casualties were decreasing; "Vietnamization" had become the official American policy; and troops were being drawn out of Vietnam at a steady pace after the Nixon administration took office. As we will see in the next section, a crucial reversal of American public opinion concerning the Vietnam War also occurred at this point, another indicator of a change in American mood about foreign affairs.

In fact, Jack Holmes, who expanded on Klingberg's early research, suggests that the end of an extrovert era might actually be characterized by excessive extroversion and likewise the end of an introvert period by excessive introversion. Thus, the point at which the reversal to a new phase takes place may exhibit excesses of the outgoing phase. Holmes suggests that the excessive period in the most recent extrovert phase be placed in the 1962-72 period, with the specific reversal marked at 1968. "This reflects the consideration that an introvert or extrovert period begins at a time when overall mood leans strongly in the opposite direction" (1977, 11). If this argument is correct, then the duration of the extrovert phase that began in 1941, as predicted by Klingberg, was rather accurate. The Vietnam War was part and parcel of the ongoing extrovert period that had begun in 1941, and that had already encompassed World War II, the Korean War, and numerous international crises and interventions involving the United States.

Certainly, the reader must be asking, such arguments cannot be taken seriously, for they imply that decision makers may be little more than mindless, overly-determined robots carrying out decisions seemingly dictated to them by some overarching mood. This critique is important, but there is a response, although it only responds in an indirect way. First, such background characteristics as moods cannot be seen as either causes or explanations of point-specific decisions or events. Thus, the fact that the United States might have been in an introverted mood did not force the decision makers to make the decisions they did on Vietnam.

Second, to suggest that decision makers are influenced by

large-scale forces is not nearly as odd as some might think, for it encompasses one of the ongoing, timeworn questions about the study of international relations: do leaders constitute the operative forces bringing about the actions, reactions, and interactions that we witness or are they merely pawns being manipulated, to some degree, by larger systems? Anatol Rapaport makes an intriguing suggestion in this regard: social (or international) systems are composed of particles, he says, and it is crucial to look at the former's effect on the latter. He suggests that the assumption that decision makers affect history may be no more sound than the assumption that "large scale social processes are determined by the interplay of forces so large that no individual's decision can significantly influence the course of events," and thus "diplo-military decisions appear *not to be the determinants of the historic process, but rather its symptoms*" (1966, 100).

There are, then, at least two questions that must be addressed, and kept separate, when considering such larger processes at work in foreign policy and international affairs. The first is whether such processes or systems can have influence; and the second is how point specific can they be, or how accurately can they pinpoint specific actions or trends? No one would argue that all decisions are dictated by any such large-scale processes, whether they be moods or others (some of which will be taken up in the next chapter). Yet it is an intriguing notion that counters the very popular view that foreign policy decision-makers operate in a vacuum, each one starting with a *tabula rasa*, and their decisions are by and large unaffected by such forces.

There is no way to test how much influence and in what domains and to what extent such larger-scale forces influence behavior, or how much latitude the decision makers have. But the Vietnam case and Klingberg's idea of alternating moods is provocative. Klingberg's evidence ended in 1950, and he argued that the then-in-existence extroverted mood would continue into the 1960s; extrapolating out using his twenty-seven year span for extrovert periods would have it ending in 1968.

Moods and Public Opinion   99

Holmes contends that the peak was in fact in 1968, with the 1968-72 period a "blow-off" of extroversion involving the American air war. Presidential symbolic rhetoric and justifications for the war peaked about 1967-68, and the troop levels and casualties decreased after 1968. While caution has been suggested about adhering too rigidly to the "average" years as generated by Klingberg, a striking finding emerges when Klingberg's data to 1950 is continued to 1984. Figure 9 presents an updating of Klingberg's measure to the present. Several conclusions emerge. First, the extrovert period that Klingberg contended began in 1941 and was still in full swing in 1950, continued with some fluctuation until 1967-68. Almost the entire 1941-67 period is higher than the previous 1919-39 period in terms of attention to foreign affairs in the State of the Union messages. Thus, this evidence demonstrates the continuation of alternating moods that Klingberg had suggested. The years 1950-68 ranged between the low 20s and the low 60s, with an average score of about 50%.

The second conclusion from this evidence is even more interesting. Beginning with the 1968 State of the Union address, and for the next eight years, the percentage of space devoted to foreign affairs remained relatively quite low.* For those eight years an average of only about 20% of the State of the Union addresses were devoted to foreign affairs. Even though President Gerald Ford's address in 1977 devoted 36% to foreign affairs, given the large fluctuations

---

*One problem that arises in using the State of the Union messages in this period is that President Nixon in four successive years (1970-73) also presented a lengthy State of the World document. These documents are not used in the present analysis (which, therefore, may understate Nixon's emphasis on foreign affairs) because one of our requirements is that the source or unit of analysis be the same for every year and every president. Nixon did not deliver a State of the World document in 1974, and Presidents Ford, Carter, and Reagan have not used such separate messages on foreign affairs. A similar problem might have occurred in 1982, when President Reagan devoted only 18% of his State of the Union message to foreign affairs, but noted that he would focus on foreign affairs "at another time." He never did so, however, at least to the extent that he focused on domestic issues in the State of the Union address.

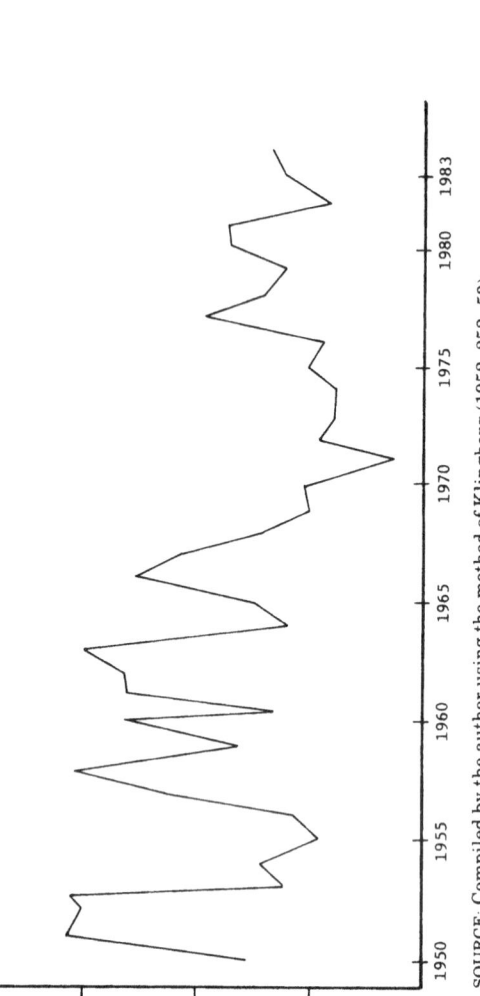

Figure 9. Percentage of the State of the Union Address Devoted to Foreign Affairs, 1950–1984

SOURCE: Compiled by the author using the method of Klingberg (1952, 252–53).

Table 4. Foreign Affairs as a Percentage of State of the Union Address, Introvert and Extrovert Phases

Introvert			Extrovert		
Dates	Years in Phase	%	Dates	Years in Phase	%
1790 - 1797	8	32	1798 - 1823	26	65
1824 - 1843	20	44	1844 - 1870	27	47
1871 - 1890	20	41	1891 - 1918	28	54
1919 - 1940	22	28	1940 - 1968	28	50
1969 - 1984	16	22			

that occur throughout the period (figure 9), that one-year increase does not represent a major shift. Moreover, subsequent to 1977, the average was roughly 25%. Even in 1982, President Ronald Reagan, although expounding a rather hawkish foreign policy tone, devoted only 18% to foreign affairs in his State of the Union address; in 1983 that increased to just above 20%, and in 1984 to almost 22%.

Table 4 reproduces Klingberg's data on the average percentage of presidential messages devoted to foreign relations during introvert and extrovert phases through 1984. For the first four introvert phases, the yearly amounts range from 27.9% to 44.2% with a mean of 36.8%; for the extrovert phases, the range is from 46.9% to 65.2%, with a mean of 56.3%. The evidence from the updated data included in Figure 9 shows that the full 1941-68 period was a fairly high 50%.

This evidence is really quite remarkable. It shows that the Vietnam War occurred during the last of several extrovert phases in United States foreign policy. Most important, just about when one would expect the phase to end, roughly twenty-two to twenty-eight years after it commenced, the State of the Union addresses began to exhibit much less interest in foreign relations than in most years during the previous twenty-seven-year period. To be sure, the Vietnam War was still in effect in 1968 and was to continue, in terms of active American involvement in the fighting, until January of 1973. But here we apparently have an anomaly, for if

Vietnam was a major foreign policy pursuit, we would have expected the State of the Union addresses to continue to focus on that important foreign policy issue. This indicator shows that foreign affairs became not nearly as important an issue as it had been for the previous generation.

Extending the data past 1968 shows that the subsequent sixteen years exhibited a rather remarkable consistency with the previous four eras of American foreign policy introversion. From 1969 to 1984, the average percent devoted to foreign affairs in State of the Union addresses was about 24%, one of the lowest of all of the introverted eras. Even were we to try to blend into these scores the amount devoted in President Nixon's State of the World presentations, the average would most likely fall within the bounds of the previous introverted eras. In 1983, despite concerted efforts to involve the United States in El Salvador, continuing unrest in Poland, the Israeli occupation of Lebanon, and the continuing occupation of Afghanistan by Russian troops, President Reagan devoted only about 22% of his State of the Union address to foreign affairs. The following year, in 1984, despite the continuation of all of the problems noted above, the killing of almost 240 American Marines in Lebanon by terrorists, and the short-lived but successful invasion of the small island of Grenada, President Reagan devoted only 26% of his State of the Union address to foreign affairs.

In other words, this unobtrusive indicator was in fact flashing an important signal by 1968 of an impending reversal in the United States' foreign policy mood, a reversal that was not to be short-lived; even during the first years of the rather bellicose Reagan administration in the early 1980s, with several international crises occurring, this indicator showed that, relatively speaking, the United States was still in an introverted mood. This indicator, therefore, did perhaps signal a shift in United States' foreign policy just about the time we would expect it to do so if the idea of alternating moods has any accuracy.

Going beyond the conclusion from what is admittedly a

rather dry, quantitative indicator, however, we can point to a number of specific events that were occurring that confirmed this signal. President Johnson announced his decision not to seek a second term and to begin peace talks with the North Vietnamese. The peak of American troop strength occurred in 1968; from then on, there was a continual and linear decline in United States' troop commitments in Vietnam. Also (a point we return to shortly), the years 1967-69 saw a significant reversal in the American public's view of the Vietnam War and of American foreign involvement in general.

Going beyond the general pattern of American foreign policy actions, however, another characteristic of introverted eras is the behavior of Congress, which tends to become obstructive in introverted eras as opposed to cooperative in extroverted stages (Roskin 1974). Figure 10 is a record of Congressional support scores from 1953-76. The last two years of the Eisenhower administration and the years 1972-76 are the lowest years of Congressional support for the president. With the exception of those two years in the Eisenhower administration, the scores from 1953 to 1971 ranged between a low of about 68% to a high of over 90%. All the scores from 1972 to 1976 are below 68%. The downward trend in the Eisenhower years is no doubt partly due to what Mueller calls the "coalition of minorities" (1973). This concept says that throughout a president's term in office more and more groups—even though each may be a small minority of the population and concerned about very different issues—can have an effect on the president's overall popularity because they all begin to oppose the president individually for not having aided their own special interest. However, this does not seem to have occurred with Kennedy from 1961 to 1963, nor Johnson from 1964 to 1968. Some deterioration seems to have occurred with Nixon from 1970 to 1973, but overall there appears to be no general tendency for such a downward curve to appear. The patterns, therefore, do not appear to be systematically a result of the coalition of minorities. The Congressional support scores actu-

Figure 10. Congressional Support for Presidential Foreign Policy, 1953–1983

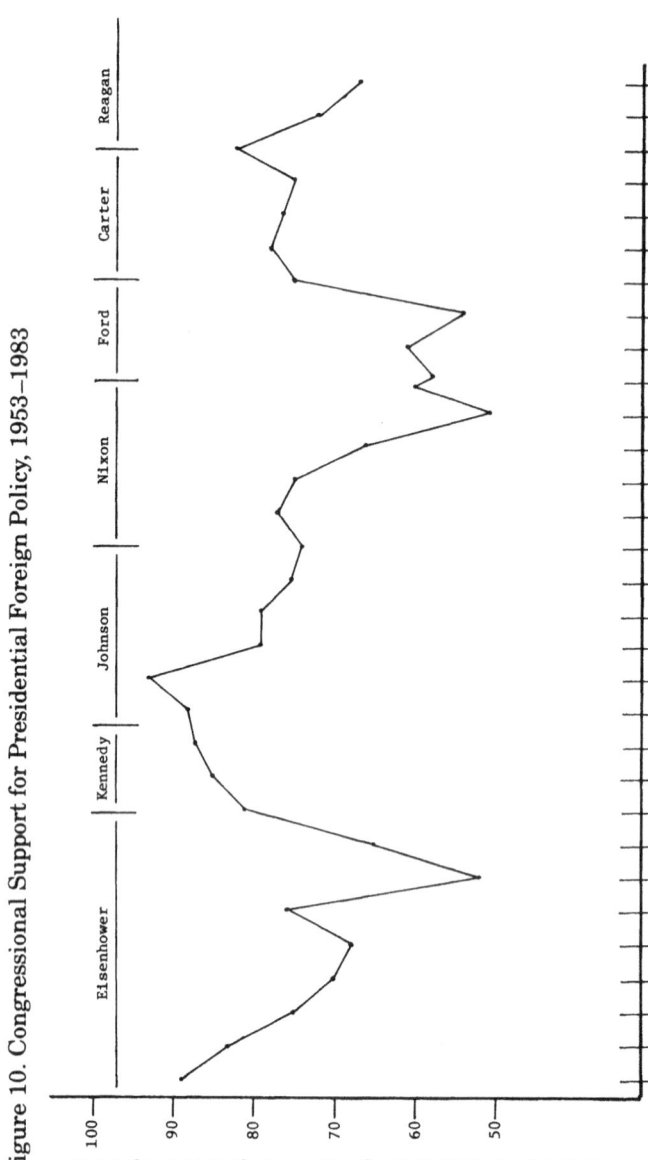

SOURCE: *Congressional Quarterly Almanac* 39:19–c.

ally increase as early Vietnam involvement increased from 1960 to 1965. That year represents a peak, with a slight drop in 1966. For six years the support is basically level; and then in 1972 there is a drop once again and for the four year period, 1973-76, the support remains very low.

These data are more difficult to interpret than the State of the Union addresses, which showed a rather clear shift just about 1967-68 for they are much more "rolling" throughout this twenty-three-year period, but nonetheless one way of assessing it is to use the 70% level as a cutoff. From 1953 through 1967, 80% of the years had scores equal to or higher than 70% support; extending this two years through 1969 shows that 82% of the years had support scores of 70% or higher. From 1968 to 1976 only 40% of the years had support scores 70% or higher, and for 1970-76, only 25% of the years fall into that category. Statistical analysis comparing the average scores in the two periods shows them to be significantly different. For 1953-67, the average support score was 78%, and in the later period the average score was 65%. While the difference is only 13%, nonetheless that difference is statistically significant; that is, a difference that large could be obtained less than one in one hundred times if we were to use simple random data. In other words, despite the fluctuations, which we would expect in this type of variable, Congress was significantly more antagonistic and less supportive of the president after 1967-68 than it had been in the 1953-67 period.

This conclusion is further supported by evidence collected by Robert J. Spitzer (1979), and reproduced here in figure 11. The dotted line in this figure represents the foreign policy bills as compared to other bills in the president's annual legislative program. That figure fluctuates between 10% and 20% from 1954 until 1971; during 1972-74 it increases to between 30% and 40%. Despite that increase in the percentage of foreign policy bills introduced, after 1968 there is a marked drop in the rate of success of those foreign policy bills. While it is impossible to say whether that decrease in the 1969-74 period was due solely to a Republican president

Figure 11. Foreign Policy Bills as a Percentage of the President's Program and Rate of Success for Foreign Policy Bills, 1954–1974

SOURCE: Calculated from Spitzer (1979, 449, 452).

dealing with a Democratic Congress, it certainly is further plausible confirmation of a change in mood. The average score of 70% success rate for 1954-67 drops to an average of 46% for 1968-74, a difference of almost 24%, which is also statistically significant.

Not only did Congress become less supportive, it also became more obstructive, especially in defense matters. Edward J. Laurance has shown that in the post-1968 period, Congress began to assert itself more, and that the Department of Defense became very concerned about this newly active role of Congress (Laurance, 1976). Figures 12 and 13 illustrate this shift. Both figures plot the number of witnesses and the number of pages of testimony advocating cuts in defense spending in Senate subcommittees on defense appropriations and Senate Armed Services Committee hearings on military procurement. The year 1969 marked a clear watershed; prior to that year, virtually no one advocated military cuts, but beginning in 1968 and surging in 1969 there clearly emerged growing opposition and contrariness. While by 1974 opposition in the Armed Services committee receded to the pre-1969 levels, Senate opposition continued to move successively higher.

All of this evidence can be brought to bear on the question of whether there has been a continuation of the pattern originally suggested by Klingberg and reiterated and analyzed by many others, and the answer seems to be yes. Sometime during the late 1960s and early 1970s United States' foreign policy did in fact revert to an introverted mood, at least relative to what that policy had been for the previous generation. A number of specific empirical indicators confirmed this. One single indicator, the amount of attention to foreign affairs contained in the annual State of the Union address, confirmed that once again the alternating introvert and extrovert moods continued.

Empirical indicators of human behavior are always hazardous to work with; nonetheless the weight of the evidence here seems to converge. When patterns repeat themselves, even very roughly, they deserve attention. American foreign policy is not static; it is very dynamic, but that dynamism and that change is not random. Patterns do exist, and this section has suggested at least one such viable pattern that can be investigated and that bears watching in terms of where we think United States foreign policy is at any specific point in time. Moreover, Vietnam fit the pattern, a conclusion that will bear on the lessons drawn from Vietnam and the implications for future United States' foreign policy.

VIETNAM AND PUBLIC OPINION

Few Americans would be surprised to learn that 66% of Americans polled in January 1974 felt that the Vietnam War had been a mistake and that it had been a mistake to

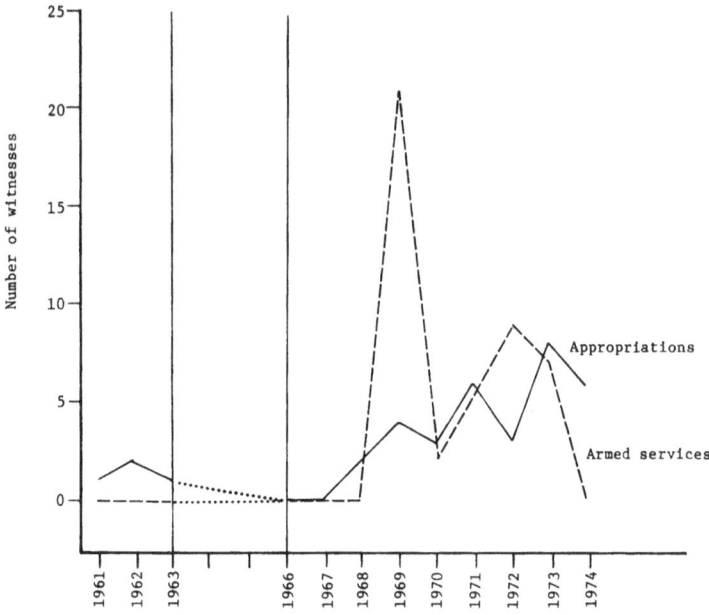

Figure 12. Witnesses Advocating Defense Cuts, Senate Armed Services Committee and Subcommittees on Defense Appropriations, 1961–1974

SOURCE: Edward J. Laurence. The Changing Role of Congress in Defense Policymaking. *Journal of Conflict Resolution* 20 (June 1976): 213–54.

send American troops to fight in Vietnam. Nor is it particularly surprising to know that by late 1970 and early 1971, 72% of Americans polled felt that of the two options of withdrawal or escalation of the Vietnam War, they chose withdrawal. These findings come as no surprise because by that time the Vietnam War had effectively ousted one United States' president and set off campus and inner-city demonstrations for and against the war that had sorely divided the country.

But the previous section indicated that by the late 1960s the overall mood of American foreign policy had effectively shifted from its previous stance of extroversion to one of introversion. Widespread negative attitudes toward the Viet-

Figure 13. Pages of Testimony Advocating Defense Cuts, Senate Armed Services Committee and Subcommittees on Defense Appropriations, 1961–1974

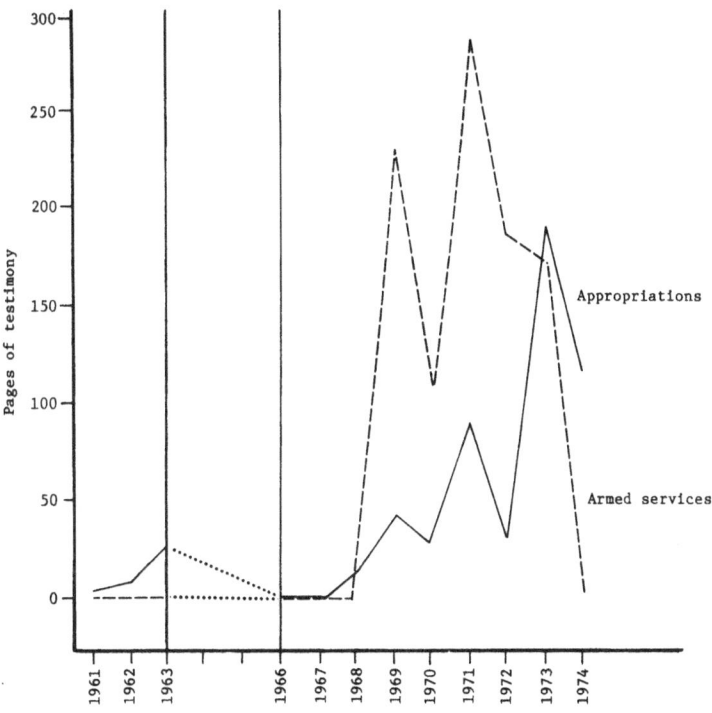

SOURCE: Laurence (1976, 227–28).
NOTE: Data for 1964 and 1965 do not appear in the source.

nam involvement are not surprising during such an introverted phase. But what was American public opinion toward the Vietnam situation prior to that shift to introversion?

Figure 14 tracks the answers to the question of whether the sending of American troops to Vietnam had been a mistake or not. By December 1966, there were 385,000 United States troops in Vietnam, over 5,000 American casualties had been incurred, and the weekly casualty rate for all of 1966 averaged almost 100. Yet only about one-third of

Figure 14. Responses to the Question, "Was Sending American Troops to Vietnam a Mistake?" 1966–1974

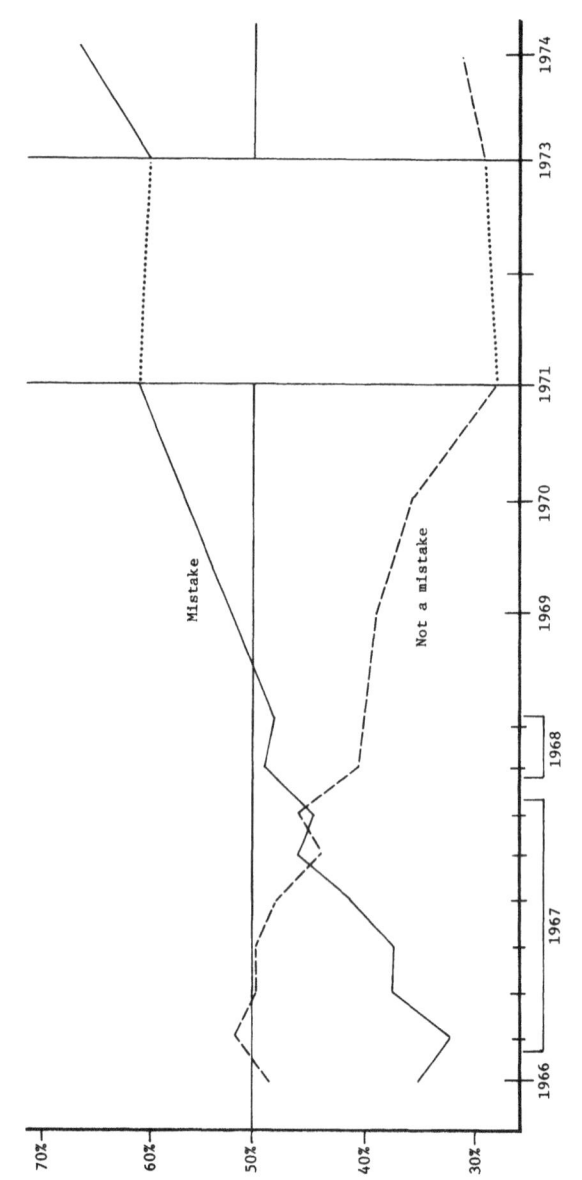

SOURCES: *The Gallup Poll, 1966–1972* (New York: Random House); *The Gallup Poll, 1973–1974* (Wilmington, Del.: Scholarly Resources, Inc.).

NOTE: No data are given for 1972, presumably because the question was not asked.

Moods and Public Opinion

Americans felt that the involvement up to that point had been a mistake, while roughly 50% felt it had not been a mistake. Even by mid-1967 there were substantially more Americans in favor of the American involvement than were opposed. By that time Secretary of Defense Robert McNamara had begun to turn against the war, had commissioned *The Pentagon Papers*, and was soon to be ousted by President Johnson because of his growing doubts. Campus teach-ins had been going on for over two years. The "dump-Johnson" movement was in its formative stages with its goal of ousting President Lyndon Johnson because of American involvement in Vietnam.

Yet, by May of 1967, 50% of all Americans polled still felt Vietnam had not been a mistake; only 38% felt the opposite. It was not until late 1967, by which time the war had been intensely prosecuted for over two years, that the percentage viewing the troop involvement as a mistake just about equalled the percentage taking the opposite position, roughly 45%. In 1968, the year Lyndon Johnson withdrew from the presidential race, the crossover finally occurred, with just under 50% thinking it had been a mistake and about 40% still maintaining it was not. It was not until May of 1969 that a majority of Americans, just over 50%, felt that the Vietnam involvement had been a mistake. Thus, while this evidence does demonstrate growing disenchantment with the war, it is also true that there was support for that involvement throughout the entire period when the major escalatory decisions for the prosecution of the war were being made.

The mistake question is a general one, and it might be of slightly questionable validity. That is, there may be a tendency to put off admitting that one has made a mistake in any endeavor. Other evidence, however, confirms what we have already seen, and does not suffer from that methodological problem. William Lunch and Peter Sperlich (1979) have brought together much of the poll evidence on Vietnam. Some can be used here.

Figure 15 reflects the trend in the percentage of Ameri-

Figure 15. Respondents Supporting Various "Withdrawal" or "Escalation" Options, 1964–1972

SOURCE: William Lunch and Peter Sperlich, American Public Opinion and the War in Vietnam. *Western Political Quarterly* 32 (March 1979), p. 26. Reprinted with permission of the University of Utah, copyright holder.

cans favoring the options of furthering escalation in Vietnam or withdrawal (Lunch and Sperling 1979, 26). From 1964 through the middle of 1969 there was never an instance when withdrawal was favored by more people than favored the escalation option. In other words, throughout the entire period when decisions were being made to further escalate the war the American public consistently favored that option over the alternative of withdrawal.

Moreover, an interesting pattern occurs in the trend of those favoring the escalation option from 1964 to 1967, a pattern which relates to the question of the role of public opinion in the formation of public policy. While registering a fairly high 45% in late 1964, the figure drops sharply to about 21% in mid-1965, remains level until the beginning of 1966, and then steadily increases to late 1967. At the same time, namely early 1966 to early 1967, the percentage of persons favoring withdrawal actually drops from just under 20% to about 5%. One obvious interpretation of this pattern is that in fact during a very crucial time, from November 1964 to about mid-1965, the American public was becoming less interested in escalating the Vietnam involvement, but through late 1965 and into 1966 the administration was able to work on public feeling about Vietnam (accounting for that flat stretch in the "escalation" option) and that such work paid off for the administration's policy with the increase in those favoring escalation subsequent to early 1966.

However, it is still important to note that throughout this whole time period the escalation option was favored by more people than favored the withdrawal option. Thus, during the very time when American leaders were making the crucial decisions to become heavily involved and to increase that involvement, and were encouraging the public to agree with them, the American public was more hawkish than dovish. This continued until late 1967, at which time almost 55% favored escalation as opposed to under 10% favoring withdrawal.

Beginning about mid-1967, the percent favoring withdrawal increased, but it was not until mid-1969 that the two figures crossed, with a larger percentage finally favoring withdrawal than escalation. But even into 1970 over one-fourth of the Americans polled still favored escalation over withdrawal, and it was not until late 1970 and early 1971 that the figures clearly show disenchantment and a move toward withdrawal. By that time, almost three-fourths of the American public favored that option.

As previously noted, the meaning of such poll data is not always explicitly apparent. It certainly was true that the public was being manipulated by the administration during this period through patriotic exhortations, controlled leaks, and lies. Nonetheless the survey data show that even into 1969, a year after the war had reached its nadir, there was support not only for United States involvement in Vietnam but even for further continuation and escalation. Disenchantment, of course, ultimately set in, as the poll data also show.

It is noteworthy that a full ten years after 50% of the American public finally supported withdrawal and only 30% supported further escalation, candidate Ronald Reagan labeled the Vietnam War a "noble cause" during his campaign for president in 1980. While certainly his statement was aimed at an appeal to voters on patriotic grounds, and was not necessarily an indicator of public readiness to immediately embark on further foreign adventures, nonetheless its use might illustrate that the growing perception of Vietnam as a disaster might easily be turned around at some future date, given the correct circumstances.

Perceptions of the American involvement in the Vietnam War as running against the so-called United States National Interest took years to evolve. The perceptions that were to emerge in the 1970s against the Vietnam involvement were in fact a product of that very involvement. In fact, Reagan's statement in 1980 should warn us against assuming that those perceptions of the 1970s represent some unshakeable attitude toward all future American foreign involvement.

Considering the general pattern of support for the war throughout those years, it is instructive to look at what groups of Americans supported it the most. Did certain classes of society most strongly support the American effort, and did other groups oppose it? John Mueller, as well as Lunch and Sperlich, present evidence concerning these questions. In light of the general view that the more educated, young, and wealthy opposed the war and that the less-educated, older, and poorer groups favored the war, their evidence is quite interesting.

First, despite the widespread campus unrest and great open opposition to the war from the young and the students in the late 1960s, there is little systematic evidence to support the contention that the young, at any time during the war, were its strongest opponents. Mueller presents the Gal-

Figure 16. Trends in Support for the War in Vietnam, by Age Group, 1965–1971

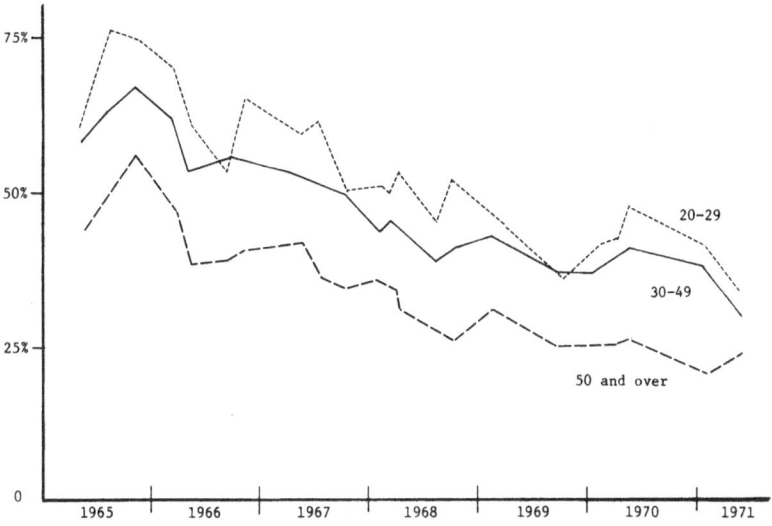

SOURCE: John Mueller, *War, Presidents, and Public Opinion* (New York: John Wiley and Sons, 1973), p. 139. Reprinted with permission of the author.

lup poll data on the mistake question from 1965 to 1971, broken down by age (figure 16). Although this may not be the best indicator of hawkishness, since it only tapped whether the respondent felt the sending of troops had been a mistake, nonetheless there is likely to be a close relationship between how one answers this question and the withdrawal-escalation questions. The youngest group, 20-29 years of age, registered the highest hawkish percentage on all but two of the nineteen occasions when this question was asked. On every other occasion but those two their percentage of "no" answers is higher than the two other age groups.

Moreover, there is a systematic relationship between age and the answer to this question: the younger the respondent, the more likely they were to say the sending of troops was not a mistake. Campus disruption and youthful opposition to the war notwithstanding, the greatest overall opposition occurred in the oldest age group. In late 1965, 75% of the youthful group felt it was not a mistake to have sent troops, compared to about 50% of the 50 and over age group. Even in May of 1970, almost one-half of the 20-29 age group (48%) still felt sending troops had not been a mistake; and by May of 1971, 34% still held that position.

The evidence for the policy alternatives of escalation or withdrawal is somewhat less accurate, for a number of reasons (see Lunch and Sperlich 1979, 33), but it also shows that in 1964, 1966, 1968, and 1970 those under 35 favored escalation over withdrawal, with only one exception: In 1966 49% of the over-35s favored escalation as opposed to 45% of the under-35s. In every other instance the under-35s favored escalation over withdrawal, with differences in percentages from 5% to 10%.

What about education and wealth? Did the poorer, less-educated (the so-called hard hats that President Nixon relied on for support) defend the war more than the wealthy and well-educated? Although the evidence is mixed, by and large the answer again is no. From 1965 through 1967 the college educated supported the war more strongly than those with a high school or grade school education (higher percentage answering no to the mistake question). The least supportive were grade school educated. From 1968, just after the Tet offensive, through 1971, the college and high school educated about equalled each other in terms of support, but again the grade school educated gave the least support.

Answers to the withdrawal-escalation options are more difficult to interpret. For withdrawal, there is no truly clear pattern, although there is a very slight curvilinear tendency for withdrawal to become less popular as education increases, but then reverse and become slightly more popular for those with advanced degrees. For escalation, that pattern is more clear, except for 1970: escalation becomes more popular the higher the education until postgraduate study, where the popularity of escalation drops drastically. Thus, if any pattern can be said to describe the response to the options by education it is a curvilinear one: the more educated the more hawkish, until a point is reached (postgraduate study) where that group turns more dovish.

For income there is a similar pattern. In 1966 and 1968, as income increased, the popularity of withdrawal actually decreased until the highest income level, when it increased. In 1970 there is a slight pattern for withdrawal to become less popular as wealth increases with no increase in popularity at the highest income level. For the escalation option, the same pattern as was found with education emerges much more clearly: as income increases the popularity of escalation increases but then reverses itself. The point of reversal differs from year to year, with the reversal occurring earlier in 1968 than the other years.

Finally, given the above evidence, it is not particularly surprising that the American elite also supported the war in its early years. In their study on the meaning of Vietnam for future American foreign policy, Holsti and Rosenau sent mail interviews to 2,503 American leaders from a wide variety of occupations. One area of their study relevant here dealt with questions about what the leadership elite felt about the Vietnam War when it first became an issue and then toward the end of United States' involvement (during the early 1970s). When the war was first an issue, 54% tended to favor a complete military victory, and only 21% favored a complete withdrawal. Toward the end of United States involvement, the figures reversed themselves, with only 24% favoring a complete military victory and 54% favoring complete withdrawal (personal communication, September 1981).

As noted already, the interpretation of this type of evidence is not completely open and shut, and relates to the question of the role of public opinion in the formation of foreign policy. On the one hand, we do know that American leaders were manipulating the public with patriotic slogans for the greater part of the war, and it is a long-held assumption in the study of American foreign policy that "polls do not make policy so much as follow policy in most areas of international affairs. . . . The President makes opinion, he does not follow it. The polls tell him how good a politician he is" (Seymour Martin Lipset cited by Lunch and Sperlich 1979, 22). Yet, on the other hand, polls are used by presidents and others to gauge the public pulse, and the implication of the evidence in this section is that the public was giving the presidents encouragement throughout the early years of the war, which did not change until after the bulk of the Vietnam damage had been done.

The public opinion poll data in this case might be read as indicating that it does influence policy decisions. When the public registered high positive feelings about the war, major decisions to escalate the war were made. Years later, when the tide had turned, and the public was showing its disfavor for the war, major de-escalatory decisions were made to extricate the United States from Vietnam. While this interpretation of a complex phenomenon is admittedly somewhat simplistic, it is one that does not contradict the empirical evidence.

We must at this point restate an important caveat: none of this evidence in any way should be seen as absolving any decision makers for making incorrect or insidious decisions concerning the Vietnam War. It is important to remember that the crucial decisions on Vietnam were not being made when the polls of 1969, 1970, and 1971 were taken, but rather when the polls of 1964, 1965, and 1966 were taken and made public. The public opinion polls of those two periods are drastically different.

CONCLUSION

This chapter has covered a broad scope, from long-term fluctuations in the moods of American foreign policy to an analysis of public opinion during the Vietnam War. The evidence on foreign policy moods is often looked upon with suspicion and disdain because of its seemingly deterministic and, some would say, atheoretical nature. Yet Klingberg's forecast made in the early 1950s based on past trends in moods were in some respects remarkably accurate.

Moreover, the evidence revealed, especially in the presidential State of the Union messages, concerning the return to introversion in the late 1960s and early 1970s, further confirms those earlier forecasts. This is not to say that the United States became isolationist in the late 1960s and early 1970s, nor did it turn totally inward then or at any time during the 1970s. The important point is that the American foreign policy stance went through a radical change just about the time one would have expected it to given certain premises in the mood notion. Moreover, that change can be effectively measured.

Furthermore, that change is reflected in survey data not strictly limited to questions about the American involvement in the Vietnam War. Watts and Free present indices constructed from people's responses to questions concerning the United States' "general posture" in the world (Watts and Free, 1976, 21). The indices are called "total internationalist," "total isolationalist," and "mixed" (figure 17). The spread between the two extreme indices was 57% in favor of internationalist in 1964, dropping to 41% by 1972, and to 19% and 21% respectively in 1975 and 1976. Clearly the perception by the American public in the mid-1970s was drastically different from their perception of the United States' role in the world in the mid-1960s, an important background factor that possibly worked toward certain types of decisions in the 1960s and against those very types of decisions in the 1970s.

After the Vietnam experience, some individuals tried to argue against the contention of a change in mood; in fact, one form of liberal response to the war itself was to contend that there was something inherently wrong in the American body politic that would automatically produce the Vietnam-type experiences. William Caspary, for instance, claimed that "the American public opinion is characterized by a *strong* and *stable* 'permissive mood' toward international involvements" (1972, 453). Caspary's data, however, consisted of answers to questions only during the 1942-55 period. He admits that he had no more current data, but then interprets the Vietnam experience itself as support for

Figure 17. Internationalist and Isolationist Opinion, 1964–1976

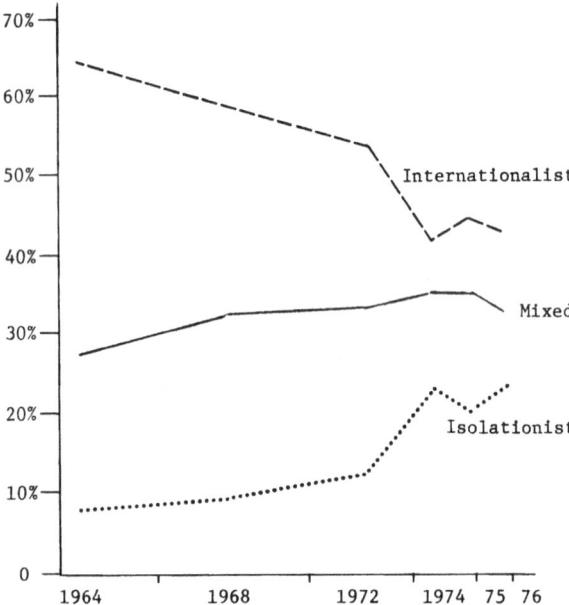

SOURCE: William Watts and Lloyd Free, A New National Survey: Nationalism, Not Isolationism. *Foreign Policy* 24 (Fall 1976): 21.

NOTE: The figures for 1964 and 1968 are derived from responses to five statements concerning the general posture the United States should assume in world affairs. The figures for 1972, 1974, 1975, and 1976 reflect responses to the same set of statements, as well as two new statements regarding possible U.S. military intervention in defense of allies.

his position. "It is tempting to speculate that the support by the long-suffering American public of ten years of fighting ... is an indication of the existence of a permissive mood ... such a mood provides a blank check for foreign policy adventures, not just a responsible support for international organization, genuine foreign assistance, and basic defense measures" (1972, 453).

We have shown here that such is not the case, and will argue in chapter 6 that much of what has transpired in

American foreign policy during a greater part of the 1970s and the early 1980s also raises questions concerning Caspary's assertions. While we have relied extensively on the unobtrusive measure of the State of the Union messages, and the amount in those messages devoted to foreign affairs, we can enumerate briefly here a number of historical incidents that also support the contention of a newly-introverted foreign policy. (1) Further aid for Cambodia in 1974-75 and for South Vietnam in 1975, as Saigon was falling to North Vietnamese forces, was vehemently rejected by the Congress and strongly opposed by the public. (2) In early 1976 the Congressional reaction to the news that the United States had aided pro-Western forces in Angola was to refuse further aid. (3) When Cuban troops and Soviet supplies were aiding the forces attacking Zaire, the United States responded by doing nothing. (4) In 1978, the United States' ambassador to Afghanistan was shot and killed in the American embassy in Kabul. Even though Russians on the spot may have condoned or even have been directly or indirectly involved in the shooting, the United States did nothing but protest. (5) Finally, the difficulty that the Reagan administration encountered throughout its first two years in office in trying to mobilize the public on the question of alleged Cuban and Russian intervention in El Salvador. This last illustrates even further the deep-rootedness of this introverted perception of American foreign policy by the public, and the lack of a strong and stable permissive mood.

The lessons about American involvement in the Vietnam War and the implications for future American foreign policy more generally should be somewhat different when these "cuts" into that involvement are taken into account. What was happening within the country and the place of American foreign policy in longer-term trends cannot be ignored if we are going to draw the widest and most relevant implications about the Vietnam fiasco, failure, quagmire, noble cause or whatever we wish to call it.

5. The Vietnam War, the Cold War, and Long-Term Trends

One goal of this work has been to broaden our view of the American involvement in the Vietnam War, and, ultimately, American foreign policy in general. The progression to this point has moved from the narrow to the broader perspective, and in so doing we have become more and more removed from the specifics of the individuals involved and of the Vietnam War itself. In this chapter we move even farther from specifics and consider several short- and long-term fluctuations in large-scale behavior of the international system, and their possible relevance to the Vietnam War. Because we are more removed from the war itself, the relevance of this evidence becomes less direct. But it must nonetheless be considered in any analysis of the war and the place of American foreign policy in that venture.

The first perspective deals with the Vietnam War and the Cold War that began in the late 1940s after World War II, and continued, some think, into the early 1970s. We address questions such as what was the relationship, if any, between the Vietnam War and the Cold War in which it was supposedly embedded? Was it part of the Cold War, did the Cold War justify American action in Southeast Asia as part of the larger containment policy, and is it true that the Vietnam War finally brought the Cold War to an end?

A second perspective focuses on international war and violence. No subject has engrossed scholars of international politics more than war, and one possibility we investigate here is the applicability of long-term cyclical variations in warlike activity in the international system. Some observers in very recent years have viewed the outbreak of major war as having low probability in the contemporary system (Sullivan and Siverson, 1981; Sullivan, 1982). Hunter argued that because of the emergence of "economic power," war between the major powers "may virtually disappear" (1972-73, 381). Morse also saw the superpowers as having become stalemated, with economic and other issues replacing the traditional military-security issues (1972, 131-32). In 1981 Werner Levi published a book with what many probably felt was a hopefully prophetic title, *The Coming End of War*. These citations are only a small number representing a very large body of literature that contended that because economic problems had come to the fore, because nations had become inextricably interdependent, and because the nature of the issues between nations had also changed, war in the contemporary system had also changed in terms of being a viable foreign policy option (Sullivan and Siverson, 1981; Sullivan, 1982).

These were not new feelings. Certainly, during the 1950s and the early 1960s, after World War II and the stalemate in Korea, many Americans felt that the United States would not again become embroiled in a major war, and yet it did. After the trauma and destruction of the Vietnam War, and with the emergence of much of the literature just noted above, Americans again seemed to feel that war was no longer a major problem. Indeed, one of the early lessons of the Vietnam War seemed to be that major war was no longer a true option for most, if not all, nations. While it is true that in 1981 and 1982 the nuclear freeze movement emerged both in the United States and Europe, clearly indicating a very strong concern about the issue of war, it is interesting that the movement's focus was, in fact, rather narrow: the concern that through either miscalculation, error, misperception, or perhaps even calculation, the major powers would engage in a nuclear exchange. There was little or no concern in the movement for war in general, even a battle involving one or more of the major powers at the subnuclear level. The implication here is that, just as in the past it has been dangerous to assume away the possibility or probability of war, likewise it may be dangerous to enlist the same assumption about contemporary international politics or, more particularly, about current American foreign policy.

A third perspective concerns the structure of the international system during the Vietnam years, and the possibility that a link can be drawn between the type of structure of the international system and the type of war that such systems might produce. What follows does not constitute a true test of any hypotheses concerning the structure of the international system and its relationship to the Vietnam War, but rather graphically and plausibly illustrates the types of links that can be drawn from scholars who have tested such hypotheses to the specific case of the Vietnam War.

This same observation applies to the fourth perspective discussed here, namely, the "world system" approach to the study of international politics, which contends that there may exist a long-term world system that can be tracked over very long periods of time, even up to five and six hundred years. According to this view, there are alternating relationships between certain core and other periphery countries, and that some types of international behavior, such as the type or character of war at any given time, can be traced to where the system is in the relations between these two types of countries and in the amount of power distributed among the major powers.

None of these large-scale perspectives is meant to explain the specific occurrence of the Vietnam War, when it occurred, or when it ended. Rather, these perspectives are an attempt to step back and put some envelopes around the Vietnam War and America's involvement in order to bring to bear the broadest possible perspective.

THE VIETNAM WAR AND THE COLD WAR

One generally and popularly accepted explanation of the United States' involvement in the Vietnam War is that it flowed from the larger Cold War pitting the two largest and most powerful nations coming out of World War II against each other. While the bipolarity that emerged in the late 1940s and early 1950s was later to fade, during much of that crucial period a popular interpretation of world politics pitted the socialist, atheist, Eastern-bloc countries against the capitalist, religiously oriented, Western countries. Although it was not a complete split (the United States even provided aid to some Eastern European, Communist-bloc countries) still the political rhetoric and popular perception at the time was of a highly bipolarized world.

It is interesting, then, to see exactly how the Vietnam War fits within that broader context of the East-West struggle. A brief historical review shows the Cold War to be not one single, static entity, but rather a changing, dynamic, fluctuating, interaction process. The six-year period from 1946 to 1952 was a relatively "hot" period in East-West relations, including the Russian takeover of Eastern Europe, the Berlin crisis of 1948, the formation of NATO, the Marshall Plan, and the outbreak of the Korean War. This was followed by a period of relative détente, from about 1953 to perhaps 1956, with the occurrence of the stalemate and then the cease-fire of the Korean War in 1953, the 1954 Geneva Conference to consider a settlement to the Vietnam situation, the Geneva summit of 1955, and the so-called Spirit of Camp David. The next hot period lasted from about 1956 to about 1963, and included the Russian invasion of Hungary in 1956, the downing of an American U-2 in Russia and the subsequent cancellation of the 1960 summit meeting, the Bay of Pigs, Kennedy's bellicose speech following his summit meeting with Khrushchev in 1961, erection of the Berlin Wall of 1961, and finally the Cuban Missile Crisis of late 1962. The one exception during this period was 1959, when there was much-heralded talk of détente between East and West, which, of course, was followed by the breakup of the planned 1960 summit meeting between Premier Khrushchev and President Eisenhower because of the Russian downing of the American U-2 spy plane.

The Vietnam War then enters the picture, a seemingly

logical outgrowth of the larger Cold War. Justified consistently as a response to "Communist aggression" by the Russians, the Chinese, or both, American action from this historical perspective appears to be just an operational manifestation of the containment policy formulated to resist the spread worldwide of Communism. Then, by the early 1970s, there was much talk again of détente by President Nixon and his national security advisor, Henry Kissinger; the secret Kissinger trip to China and the two Nixon trips to Peking and Moscow seemed to herald yet another shift in the fluctuations of the Cold War.

It is interesting, however, to compare this rough historical overview with somewhat harder and possibly more objective evidence concerning the events that transpired during this Cold War period and see in what way the Vietnam War did—or, more importantly, did not—fit the above description. In the historical chronology outlined here, we relied on certain important events that occurred during the period of the Cold War. But note that we used only a few, most likely key events, and the problem with that method is the common human fallacy of selectivity. In recent years, scholars have begun to rely on a technique labeled "events data analysis," a method by which the scholar uses every reported event during the time period of interest, thereby obtaining a much more complete historical chronology. While there are certainly some methodological issues still unresolved in the use of such evidence,* nonetheless it has proved its worth in scores of studies.

Several different ways exist for presenting this evidence, and each one gives a slightly different picture. The Cooperation and Peace Data Bank (COPDAB) codes the events that appear in the daily newspaper along a thirteen-point scale for conflict and cooperation, so that each event, in addition to being recorded as cooperative or conflictual, is given a score for intensity. Figure 18 presents the sum of all United States-Russian conflict intensities minus the sum of all their cooperative intensities, by year, from 1948 to 1973

*See Azar (1973); Burgess and Lawton (1972); Azar, McClelland, and Brody (1972); Howell (1983); Vincent (1983); McClelland (1983).

Figure 18. Intensity of Conflict and Cooperation Behavior, United States-USSR, 1948-1973

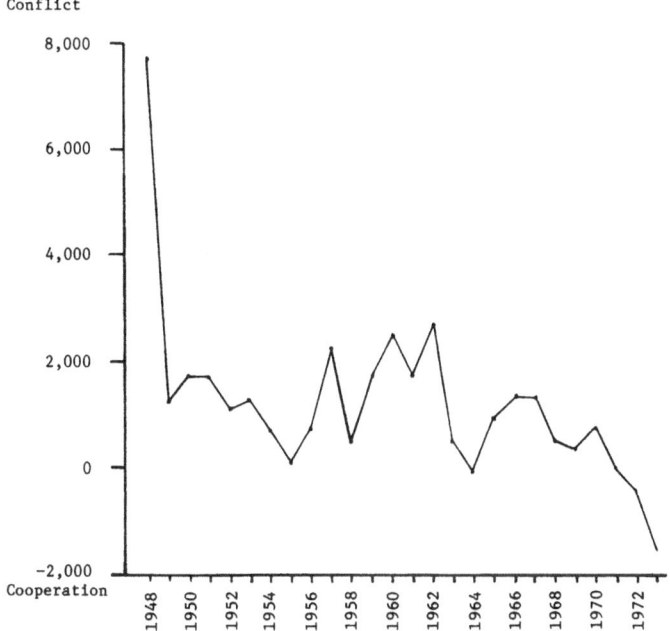

SOURCE: Edward Azar and Thomas J. Sloan. *Dimensions of Interaction: A Source Book for the Study of Behavior of 31 Nations from 1948 to 1973.* Occasional Paper no. 8, International Studies Association. Pittsburgh: University of Pittsburgh Center for International Studies, 1975.

(Azar and Sloan 1975). The chart shows an overall move toward more cooperation from 1948 to 1973, with very low points of conflict reached in 1955, 1958, 1964, and finally 1971-73. The fluctuations in figure 18 do not reflect the neat picture outlined in the historical chronology, but there are some similarities. Forgetting for the moment the year 1948, which included the very prolonged and intense Berlin Blockade crisis, the years 1949-53 are somewhat higher in conflict than 1954-56. The situation deteriorates up to 1962 and the Cuban Missile Crisis. The years 1963-64 show more cooperative behavior, followed by a very slight increase in conflict from 1965 to 1967, but an increase that hardly ap-

Figure 19. United States-USSR Relations, 1948–1978

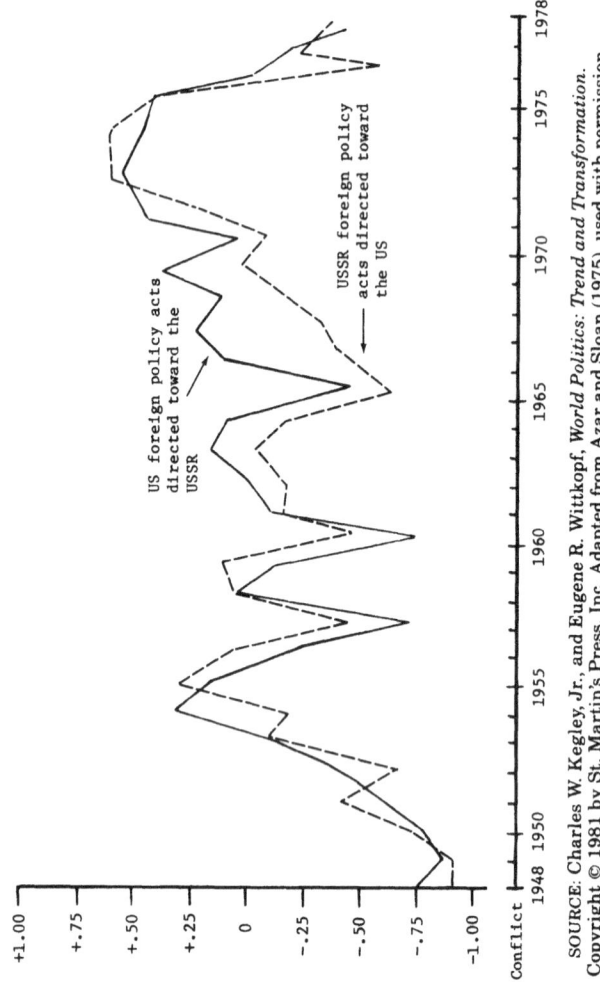

SOURCE: Charles W. Kegley, Jr., and Eugene R. Wittkopf, *World Politics: Trend and Transformation.* Copyright © 1981 by St. Martin's Press, Inc. Adapted from Azar and Sloan (1975), used with permission.

NOTE: This index is obtained by summing the proportion of cooperative acts (+%) and conflictual acts (−%). For example, if in a given year the United States directed 100 acts toward the USSR, 75 of which were cooperative and 25 conflictual, the index would be .75 − .25 = .50.

proaches the early 1960s, let alone 1948. Beginning in 1968, there is a steady move toward the cooperative end of the spectrum, with a clear crossover occurring for the first time in the twenty-six-year span of this data in 1971-72.

The events data evidence presented in this way charts the intensity of United States-Russian conflict and cooperation with each other. It shows no clear linear move toward more cooperation and détente, nor does it show an all-out, steady level of conflict behavior. Rather, United States-Russian relations exhibit a shifting pattern. Of special note here, however, in taking the entire twenty-six-year time span into consideration, is the 1961-70 period. The Cuban Missile Crisis is clearly the reason for the peak in 1962, but then in 1963-64, when Vietnam was beginning to emerge as a focal point of America's foreign policy of containment, there is greater cooperation than in 1960 and 1961. There is a slight move toward more conflict during 1965-67, but no significant change in overall United States-Russian relations during those years, the most escalatory years of the Vietnam War. Indeed, figure 18 suggests, if anything, that the war was occurring within a long-term fluctuating cooperative period between the two superpowers, and that even despite the direct prosecution of the war by the United States and direct support of North Vietnam by Russia, each side was extremely reluctant to allow the war to spill over into generalized United States-Russian relations.

This finding is confirmed and strengthened if we look at only the frequencies of cooperative and conflictual actions by the United States and the Soviet Union. Charles Kegley and Eugene Wittkopf developed a "net conflict index" by summing the proportion of cooperative acts and the proportion of conflictual acts. Thus, if in a given year the United States sent 100 acts to the Soviet Union with 75 cooperative and 25 conflictual, the United States' score for that year would be $.75 - .25 = .50$ (Kegley and Wittkopf 1981, 47).

The trend in figure 19 is similar to that of figure 18, with several exceptions, especially the year 1948 and several slight deviations in the mid-1960s. However, both figures show an overall move toward greater cooperation into the early 1970s. The year 1963, with the signing of the Partial Test Ban Treaty, had shown a peak of cooperation from the trough of 1960. A reversal then set in with the Tonkin Gulf incident of 1964 and the military buildup in Vietnam beginning in 1965.

But once again, the escalation of the Vietnam War did not disrupt this overall generalized move toward more cooperation in United States-Russian diplomatic relations. In fact, the years 1966-73 showed a surge toward more cooperation, similar to 1949-55. What is most amazing in figure 19 is the period subsequent to 1965. During the major escalation and prosecution of the war (1966-69), there were continuing increases in cooperation, with very slight reversals for the United States in 1968. With President Nixon inaugurated in 1969, the trend continued toward more cooperation into 1973, even though the Nixon administration, within an overall de-escalatory policy, actually widened the war into Cambodia and Laos. These data yield the conclusion that the Vietnam War occurred despite continuing increasing cooperation between the two main antagonists of the Cold War, and despite the fact that the Vietnam War was alleged to be part of the larger Cold War.

It should be noted that the same finding does not occur if we look at the United States-China dyad. But this may not contradict the conclusion presented. That is, the USA-PRC dyad showed a marked increase in conflict in 1965 and 1966, followed by a relative decline through 1969, an increase in 1970, and then another decline in 1971 and 1972 with the onset of rapprochement between the two countries. (This description reflects a summation of the intensity of conflict behavior minus intensity of cooperation behavior.) While this might at first raise questions about the conclusion concerning the effect of the Vietnam War on the Cold War, investigation of further data suggests that it does not. That is, China became belligerent to a number of other countries during the late 1960s. Data from Azar and Sloan (manipulated as in figure 18, but not presented here) show that re-

Long-Term Trends   131

lations between China and Russia also became intensely conflictual during the 1965-69 period, and then reversed itself to more cooperation, relatively speaking, in the early 1970s. The late 1960s was the period of the Cultural Revolution in China, and, given the similarity in the pattern of PRC-USA and PRC-USSR behavior, we can probably conclude that it was that factor that produced increased United States-Chinese hostility during the late 1960s rather than the American involvement in the Vietnam War.

As a methodological footnote, it should be noted that these conclusions are not data-specific; that is, they are not the result of the use of one data source or type of manipulation. Ashley (1980) has presented data on the relations between these three major powers from similar sources but manipulated in much different ways, and yet the conclusions are remarkably similar. Ashley did not use frequency counts (figure 18) or proportions of conflictual to cooperative events (figure 19). Rather, he coded his data along a thirty-point scale of intensity. He presented his events data in three ways: the average conflict-cooperation intensity by year, the highest conflict in the year, and the highest cooperative act in the year. The first two are the most meaningful because they show, in most instances, the greatest variations.

For the United States-Russian dyad (Ashley 1980, 93-94), there is a slight increase in conflict in 1965 in both the peak and mean scores, but then in both cases the trend is either down or level through the entire course of the rest of the Vietnam War. The same holds true for the United States-Chinese dyad, with the highest point of conflict (whether using the peak action or the mean score) being 1965, followed by a rather steady trend down in conflict throughout the rest of the Vietnam War. It is interesting that of the three dyads in the Ashley data, the Russian-Chinese is the only one that shows an actual increase in conflict throughout most of the 1964-70 period. Although that description differs in accuracy depending on whether one focuses on the peak or mean score, and on which way the action is directed

(Soviet Union toward China or vice versa), of the three dyads, the one undergoing the least disintegration, the one becoming more harmonious and less conflictual, is the United States-Russian dyad.

Broadening the arena even further to East-West relations in general, the same conclusion is justified. Kjell Goldmann generated what he called a measure of "East-West Tension in Europe." It is similar to events data, but different in that it consists of statements by leaders in the NATO and Warsaw Treaty Organization countries that appear in public sources, rather than events. Although the data exclude any statements by United States leaders about non-European affairs, all statements concerning European affairs or directed at or relevant to one or more of the East European countries are included. Thus, while the coefficient does reflect tensions in Europe, it is not a measure of worldwide tensions, nor is it necessarily reflective of tensions in other parts of the world. Since there seemed to be a great deal of concern during the Vietnam War that Cold War activities in that region might spill over into other areas of the world, it would behoove us to investigate this measure.

Several conclusions immediately catch the eye (figure 20). First, the trend in European tensions, as with previous data, grows more cooperative throughout the 1948-70 period. Second, and again similar to previous data, the trend toward more cooperation is not strictly linear. Rather, clear deviations around that trend are present, and those deviations reflect the historical description presented earlier in this chapter even more so than with the actual events data just presented. There was a hot period from 1946 to 1952, a cooling off of tensions lasting at least until about 1956, a slightly more hostile period from 1957 to 1963 (with a major exception again being 1959) followed by a period of more cooperative behavior lasting from 1964 to 1970, once again with the marked exception of 1968. The respective periods as reflected in these data last for 7, 4, 7, and 7 years, and the respective mean scores on Goldmann's index for those four periods are $-.51$, $-.06$, $-.40$, and $.31$ (see horizontal

Figure 20. Goldmann's Coefficient of Imbalance for East-West Tension in Europe

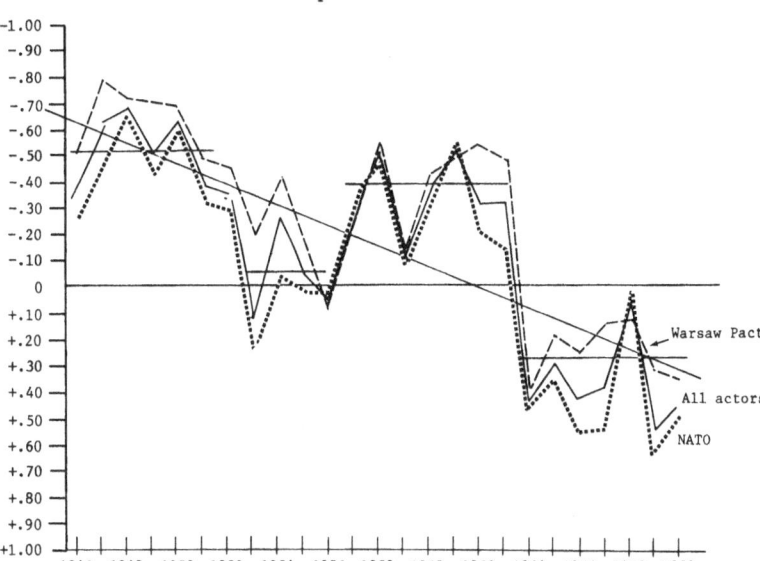

SOURCE: Reprinted by permission from Kjell Goldmann, East-West Tension in Europe, 1946–1970: A Conceptual Analysis and a Quantitative Description. *World Politics* 26 (October 1973): 118. Downsloping trend line and four horizontal lines have been added.

bars in figure 20). While the overall trend for the twenty-five-year period was toward more cooperation, fluctuations around that basic trend are split into hot and cold periods.

A final conclusion from figure 20 is that, as with the events data, tensions in Europe appear almost unaffected by the Vietnam War, and the overall move toward greater cooperation continues with only a few slight missteps. The years 1964 to 1970 were much less tension filled than at any time in the previous fifteen years, and markedly less so than the previous seven years. To be sure, beginning with 1965, there were increased perceptions of tension on the part of the Warsaw Pact nations, peaking in 1968, but that increase was in fact one of the less marked shifts in the entire twenty-five years. Moreover, it reached nowhere near the same level of tension as during the two previous peaks, nor did it in any way interrupt the overall trend toward perceptions of less tension in Europe. In addition, it was not matched by the NATO members, and therefore overall perceptions of tension in Europe (all actors) remained relatively steady, with the one exception of 1968 (the year of the Russian invasion of Czechoslovakia). After 1968 there was a move again toward perceptions of less tension.

We reach the seemingly paradoxical conclusion that the Vietnam War erupted in the context of growing cooperation between the two major powers as well as decreasing tension between the blocs in Europe. Despite the continuation and escalation of the war, the movement toward détente and cooperation was not seriously disrupted. One would have expected, given the East-West alliance structure in the 1960s, that the war in Indochina would have strongly affected East-West relations as well as direct United States-Russian relations, and yet such an expectation is not borne out by the empirical evidence. Figures 21 to 23 do not show anything near the step-level changes that we might have expected given two facts: (1) that the United States was fighting a war with a country very closely aligned with both of its major adversaries, and (2) that one publicly stated concern throughout much of the Vietnam War on the part of some United States' decision makers and public opinion makers was that either or both of those countries would enter the war on the side of the North Vietnamese.

The Vietnam War was widely justified and interpreted at the time, and since, as both an integral part of the larger Cold War and a function of the existence of the Cold War. The containment philosophy was thus justified as a reaction to what was perceived as the incorrect "appeasement" policy of Chamberlain in the late 1930s. As one wit jokingly asked, "Do you want to know why we are in Vietnam? We're in Vietnam to keep Hitler out of Czechoslovakia!" Seen in this light, of course, the war appears to be a justified, rational response to a threat. But there have been doubts raised about that interpretation (chapter 3) and in some ways the present data does the same. First, this evidence supports the idea that the Cold War was not one entity, but rather a fluctuating relationship, alternating between hot and cold periods, but with an underlying trend toward more cooperation between the United States and Russia and fewer overall perceptions of tension in Europe. The Vietnam War was an anomaly with respect to that larger Cold War: it almost doesn't show up on the charts when we track the larger Cold War.

In fact, figures 18 to 20 suggest the intriguing possibility that the Russians, East Europeans, and other Communist nations recognized that the American involvement in Vietnam diverged from the overall growing cooperation and easing of tensions. Perhaps they concluded that the war was a function, at least to some degree, of the quicksand, incremental decision making in which the American decision makers were involved and from which they could not extricate themselves. Although not citing the evidence presented here, Weinstein and Lewis conclude concerning the final victory of the North Vietnamese in Saigon: "The immediate Soviet and Chinese public reaction to the communist victory in South Vietnam were, given the magnitude of the event, cautious and ambiguous. There was no indication that either Moscow or Peking expected any direct payoffs: neither power could be sure how the victory would affect its overall position vis-à-vis the other in Indochina" (Weinstein and Lewis 1978, 130). If the Russian and Chinese decision makers did not think along those lines, then what explains why United States-Russian relations and tensions in Europe did not become much more exacerbated than they did? With the evidence in hand we cannot really answer that question; but this suggestion is certainly an intriguing one and is consistent with the data.

INTERNATIONAL VIOLENCE

Now we turn to the question of where the Vietnam War fits into longer-term fluctuations in international violence at the global, systemic level. War has always been the subject of greatest concern to scholars of international relations. Numerous perspectives and theories exist that are used to explain the outbreak, duration, intensity, and termination of war (Sullivan 1976; Sullivan and Siverson 1981 and 1983). Here the concern is not with spelling out or testing these theories, but rather viewing the separate and distinct decisions made by individual decision makers as playing a crucial part in the final option to go to war, and seeing those decisions as taking place within larger structural perspectives.

If we treat the entire international system as an observable unit, such as the stock market, we can then suggest that international war and violence can be viewed in the aggregate, just as we might treat the movement of the stock market averages or the economy as large-scale, aggregated phenomena. In other words, on any given day some stocks increase in value and some decrease, but overall the market can be viewed as one single behavioral manifestation of thousands and perhaps millions of discrete decisions. The market "went up" or the market "went down" is the way analysts describe the daily behavior of all those decisions made by a multitude of individual investors. Likewise, economic phenomena such as the consumer price index, installment debt, overall consumer debt, mortgage interest rates—all are a function of millions of individual decisions. Yet the results of those decisions, in the aggregate, can be tracked, and, claim the economists, understood as an aggregate phenomenon.

In fact, in the previous section we treated all the thousands of decisions made throughout a given year by individual national foreign policy decision makers as amenable to the same type of analysis: all those individual decisions and actions were aggregated into an overall summary of the behavior of those individuals for any given year. It became fairly clear, also, that the behavior was not an erratic or random thing; figures 18 through 20 showed some interesting long-term patterns.

What does the international system look like in terms of warlike behavior and violence? Are there patterns in the fluctuations of that behavior, or does it exhibit more randomness than pattern? Of the many questions we can ask about this phenomenon, two will be of interest here: (1) Is there any trend or pattern in war? Is international violence increasing, decreasing, or remaining just about the same? (2) Is international violence cyclical?

One of the early systematic analyses of these questions came from the Correlates of War project. Separating the 1815 to 1965 period at the century mark, they found that the number of wars went down for the second half of the period, and declined even more if they controlled for the number of nations in the system, but the opposite was the case for the magnitude and severity of war. "That is, the number of nation-months and battle deaths rises sharply for both the raw and the normalized figures. But this holds only for all international wars and for the interstate war subset; extra-systemic wars, conversely, decline not only in frequency, but in the total number of nation months and battle deaths arising from these wars" (Singer and Small 1972, 189).

Even using a finer time period distinction, namely, dividing the 150 years into five periods of thirty years each, the number of wars generally fluctuated around the mean; but again, controlling for the number of nations, the frequency of war generally trended downwards. For nation-months and battle deaths, there is an upward trend, except for extrasystemic wars.

Singer and Small's overall conclusion was that war was not increasing.

> The answer would seem to be a very unambiguous negative. Whether we look at the number of wars, their severity, or their magnitude, there is no significant trend upward or down over the past 150 years. Even if we examine their intensities, we find that later wars are by and large no different than those of earlier periods. . . .That is, the

number of interstate wars per decade has risen no faster than the number of nations in the interstate system, and the number of extra-systemic wars has declined no faster than the number of extra-systemic nations in the world (1972, 201).

Jack Levy carried out a later analysis (1980), covering the longer time period of 1495 to 1975. Levy isolated 119 wars, starting with the War of the League of Venice (1495-97), and ending with the Vietnam War (1965-73). All of the wars involved one or more of the Great Powers. Levy generated several different measures of warlike activity, including duration, extent (number of nations), magnitude (combination of extent and duration), severity (deaths), intensity (battle deaths/population), concentration (battle deaths/nation-years of war), and frequency.

Given the long time span and the large number of war dimensions, Levy's analysis is obviously extensive, and only the briefest summary can be given here. He found that wars were getting shorter, but that there was a marked increase in the "concentration," or the battle deaths occurring in any given nation-year of war. There was neither an increase nor a decrease in the extent, magnitude, severity, or intensity. For the Great Power wars, however, there was a significant increase in extent, magnitude, severity, intensity, and concentration, but no change in the duration. "It may be fair to argue that the most severe wars of any age are becoming increasingly destructive in terms of loss of life. With respect to the general question of historical trends in war, however, we must conclude that the severity of war is increasing, but at an extremely slow rate" (1980, 18).

The frequency of war has been declining over time, and the decline in the frequency of Great Power war is even greater than when considering all wars. "It appears that one of the most pronounced changes in war over the last five centuries is the abrupt decline in the frequency of Great Power war. It should be noted that this trend has been underway long before the 20th century, and thus cannot be attributed exclusively (or even primarily) to the uniqueness of this century or the emergence of nuclear weapons" (1980, 22). There has also been a decrease in the amount of war under way, including the number of wars underway at any one time, the number of Great Power wars, the number of powers at war, and the magnitude, severity, and concentration of war underway.

Levy's conclusion is quite clear: "In general, war has been diminishing over time" (1980, 27). This is true, with few, but important, exceptions. The yearly amount of war has been increasing only in the sense that the "bloodiest years are getting bloodier—absolutely, as a proportion of the population, and for each Great Power" (1980, 27). Wars are becoming shorter, slightly lower in magnitude, much greater in concentration, and unchanged in terms of severity and intensity. The most severe wars, however, are becoming more severe and intense. And while Great Power wars are becoming less frequent, those that do occur are more severe, intense, and concentrated, as well as somewhat greater in magnitude.

A number of observers contended through much of the 1970s that war had become outmoded as a viable means of a country's foreign policy (see Sullivan, 1982), and Levy's research lends some credence to that. Later research by Small and Singer divided the 1816 to 1977 period into seven smaller periods, with the two most recent being 1946-65 and 1966-77. They found that on six of eight "normalized" indicators of war (controlling for number of years in each period and the number of nations), the two most recent periods ranked the lowest and next to lowest on warlike violence (Small and Singer 1979, 104). Combining the eight indicators into an overall index shows that the last period, 1966 to 1977, was the least conflictual, and the 1946-65 period the fifth least conflictual.

Most of this evidence, therefore, points in the direction of less war over time. Looking at the data in another way, and comparing the current era with previous eras, it is possible to discern some over-time variation, perhaps even cyclical-

Figure 21. Annual Amount of International War Underway, 1816–1980

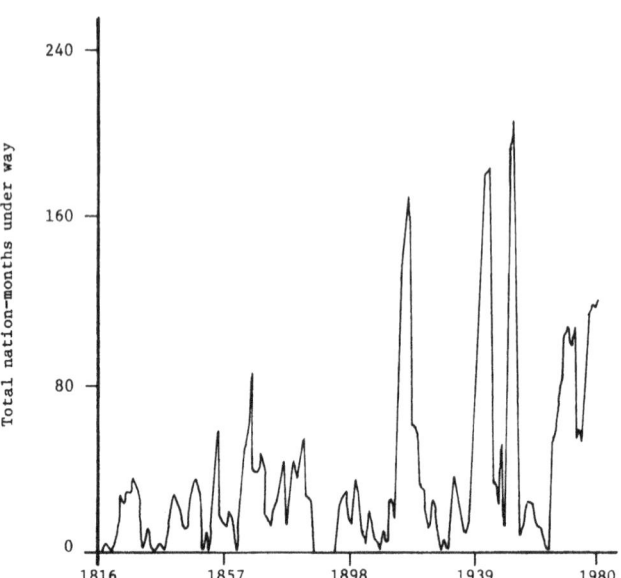

SOURCE: Melvin Small and J. David Singer, *Resort to Arms: International and Civil Wars, 1816–1980*, p. 150. Copyright 1982 by Sage Publications Inc. Reprinted by permission.

ity, in warlike behavior. Figures 21 and 22, respectively, present the nation-months of international war underway and casualties from international wars from 1820 to 1980, collected by the Correlates of War project (Singer and Small 1972, 1982). Nation-months of war underway is "nothing more than the sum of all the participating nations' separate months of active involvement in each war" (Singer and Small, 1972, 43).

At first glance the Vietnam War as depicted in figure 21 simply continues the picture of fluctuating hostilities from 1820; on only eight occasions does the series descend to about the zero level and on only three of those occasions—the 1830s, the late 1880s and early 1890s, and then again briefly in the late 1920s—does the curve remain at or near that level for any length of time. On numerous occasions, as the indicator reached the zero level, it signalled an impending increase. Likewise, in figure 22, in four out of seven cases where the casualty level reaches zero for any five-year period, the next five-year period shows an increase. Only around 1820, the mid-1830s, and 1890 does the indicator remain at the zero level for more than one five-year period. (Moreover, figure 22 shows that on six of eight occasions when the indicator reached a level of 2.00 or greater, it declined to the zero level within the next two five-year periods.)

More important, these fluctuations in violence are not random. Singer and Small at first found periodicity in the amount of war underway "with dominant peaks about 20 years apart." They concluded, "not so much that discrete wars come and go with some regularity, but that, with some level of such violence almost always present, there are distinct and periodic fluctuations in the amount of the violence" (1972, 215).

Denton and Phillips also present data generally supportive of the hypothesis that "an upswing in violence occurs about once every generation to a generation and a half, if one assumes some change in the life spans making up the 'generation'" (1968, 190). While over the period of their study (1481 to 1900) the twenty-five-year cycle fits the best, "the data support such a general trend with 20 years providing a 'best' fit prior to 1680 and about 30 years thereafter" (1968, 193).

In their later work, Small and Singer pull back from their earlier conclusion, and at first contradict Denton and Phillips. "If we define periodicity in terms of peaks and valleys of approximate magnitude, occurring at more or less equal intervals, we find no evidence for such a claim. Even using spectral analysis methods, which are explicitly designed to *find*, no less confirm, any clear cyclical patterns, we turned up nothing of significance" (1979, fn. 5). Levy agrees with this conclusion. After citing others, he contends "The absence of empirical support in the literature for the hypoth-

Figure 22. Log Transformations of Battle Deaths in International and Interstate Wars Begun per Five-Year Period, 1816–1980

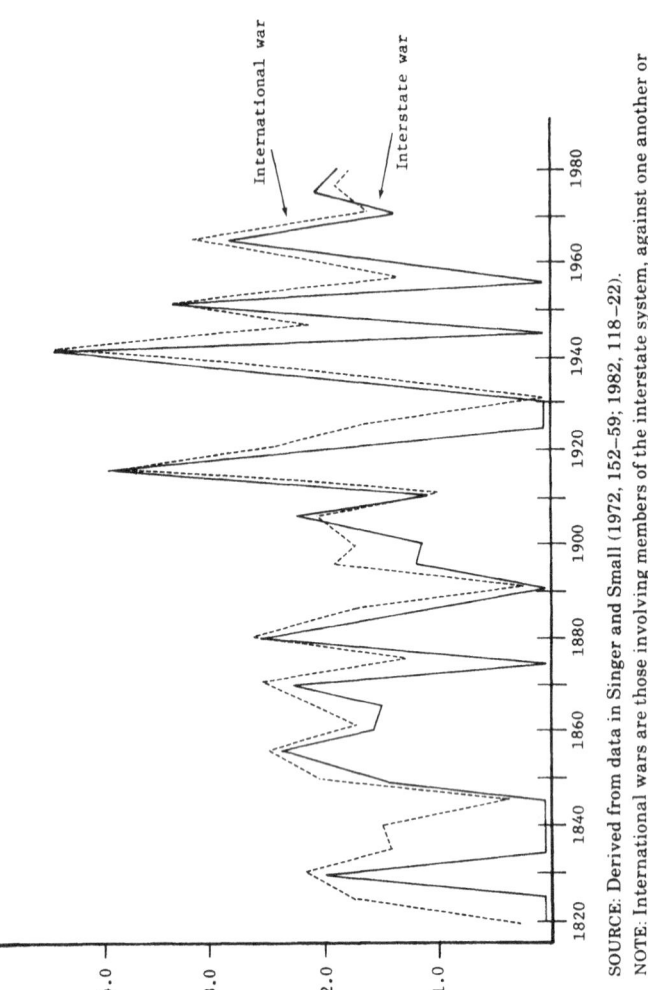

SOURCE: Derived from data in Singer and Small (1972, 152–59; 1982, 118–22).

NOTE: International wars are those involving members of the interstate system, against one another or against a nonmember; interstate wars include only the wars that had at least one system member on each side. The log transformation technique is used when certain data, such as those for World Wars I and II, are extreme cases that otherwise would dominate the graphs.

Long-Term Trends

eses of cyclical trends in war is confirmed by a visual inspection of the scattergrams presented earlier in this chapter. There are no hints of any cyclical patterns in either the occurrence of war or in any of its other dimensions. For each of the war indicators, the highest peaks in war as well as the periods of no war appear to be scattered at random" (Levy 1983, 137). Nonetheless, Singer and Small concluded that there seems to be a "rather rough, but visible, periodicity in these data over the entire 160 odd years. . . . It will be recalled that on many of the indicators, the relative peacefulness of the Concert period gave way to the extreme violence of the 1850s and 1860s, followed by a general decline in martial activities in the 1870s and 1880s. Then we experienced general increases in those activities through World War I, a decline during the inter-war years, and increases again after World War II. Finally, we have the relative decline that we have already described" (1979, 107).

If we consider roughly the mid-to-late 1930s as the beginning of one upswing of violence in this century then the next upswing would have occurred roughly around the mid-1960s, or the beginning of the increased escalation of the Vietnam War. Not unlike Klingberg's explanation of moods (1952) is Denton and Phillip's use of the well-known generational hypothesis that certain periods more readily "allow" violence to occur, and that violence may then grow until "reaction against violence per se occurs. This reaction results in lower conflict in the system until conditions permit the growth of new conflict" (1968, 190-91).

One might almost take these data to conclude that the Vietnam War tragically confirmed, in the roughest fashion, the continuing fluctuation of violence in the international system. No war *had* to happen in the mid-1960s, the United States did not *have* to be one of the protagonists. And yet, once again, despite having what David Halberstam labeled "the best and the brightest" involved in making United States foreign policy during many of those years, and despite the presence of nuclear weapons and the changed nature of the modern, interdependent international system, the rough curves plotted out from 1820 to 1965 were continued in the form of the Vietnam war.

In spite of the fact that the Vietnam involvement might have later been viewed as an aberration in terms of rational, logical, and moral decision making, still, it did happen, and it happened when one might—given the evidence presented here—expect something like that to happen. Despite its possibly aberrant nature, the Vietnam War did continue, in the most general way, the longer-term fluctuations in international violence. While this evidence does not yield implications specifically relevant to the Vietnam involvement, it does suggest that attention to such fluctuations and possible rough periodicities in large-scale behavior at the level of the international system bears investigation and monitoring.

SYSTEM CONFIGURATION

Although decision makers and, in democratic systems, the public bear the ultimate responsibility for the actions of their governments, it would be myopic and narrow-minded to assume that either decision makers or the public have total control over what happens in the international system. There has been a long-running and unsettled debate over whether decision makers affect what happens in the system, or whether the structure of the system affects their behavior.

These long-standing debates have focused by and large around the merits and demerits of bipolar, multipolar, concentrated, or dispersed types of international systems (Sullivan 1976). On the one hand, proponents of bipolar systems contend the rigidity of such systems means that nations, and especially the major powers, will not run the risk of a major-power confrontation and possible war because of the potential devastation. On the other hand, proponents of multipolar systems see bipolar systems as dangerous because of the very possibility of that major-power confrontation. Multipolar systems, they say, produce stability because of the greater interaction opportunities afforded more of the nations: any two nations are less likely to be able to permit a confrontation between them to escalate, because they have so many other considerations in the international system due to all the other nations they must attend to.

Debates have also ranged over the respective effects of concentrated or dispersed power in the system. Proponents of concentrated systems contend that the more concentrated the system, the more certain everyone is about the various power configurations, and this certitude will produce fewer crises, and, possibly, wars, because nations know what the pecking order is. The closer a system moves toward hegemonic power, the more that one power can control what happens in the system and keep things under control. On the other hand, dispersed systems are seen as having some of the same attributes as multipolar systems: nations have to pay so much attention to other powers with equal or almost equal power that no confrontation is allowed to get out of hand. The important point is that the configuration of the overall international system affects the specific decisions of the individual decision makers, and is not to be seen as something that is so abstract and high-level that it cannot possibly impact on individual decisions. But we cannot settle these debates here, and what has been presented represents only a brief summary of the arguments on both sides.

What type of international structure existed as the Vietnam situation began to unfold? Regardless of the measures we use to represent power, two nations were clearly dominant, the United States and the Soviet Union. (Some have suggested that the system was not bipolar for a large part of the postwar period [Modelski, 1974, 8-11]. Nonetheless, it is clear that the system was not a multipolar one.) Within this basically bipolar world, several changes were taking place. First, throughout the post-World War II years the two major powers were becoming more equal in power; the evidence strongly suggests this, whether one looks at overall military spending or nonmilitary power factors such as population, industrial development, and military manpower.

Second, measured in terms of transactions between nations, this bipolar world was, beginning in the early 1950s, becoming less bipolar, although it was not until the early 1970s that bipolarity finally broke down. This was indicated at the time by the dual visits of President Nixon to China and to Russia in 1972. In the late 1950s the system still resembled more clearly a bipolar system than any other type.

The behavior characteristic of a bipolar system, in particular warlike behavior, is revealed by the evidence. Early findings from the Correlates of War project indicated that bipolarity (measured by the number of alliance formations in the system) was related to war, but that the relationship changed from one century to the next (Singer and Small, 1968). In the 19th century, more bipolarity was related to less war, while in the 20th century, the relationship vanished for the most part. McGowan and Rood found that the formation rate of alliances in the latter part of the 1895-1914 period fell off, and confirmed their hypothesis that such a decline in the systemic rate of alliance formation after 1909 indicated that the system was becoming less flexible and more bipolar, resulting in major system-changing events (1975). Their forecast was that such declines in alliance formation at other times would also result in major system-changing events.

Perhaps most relevant to the present discussion are Haas's findings concerning the different types of warlike behavior to be expected in different types of systems. He found that almost all types of systems, except unipolar ones, experienced war, but that bipolar systems tended to have few, localized, and prolonged wars. Tripolar and multipolar systems had the highest number of wars and war casualties (Haas 1970, 121; Haas 1974, 367, 381, 385, 389, 403, 416-17).

Michael Wallace also found a relationship between system polarization and war (1973). He found war more likely at very low and very high levels of polarization, and minimized at moderate levels. Partly confirming some of these findings is the research by Bueno DeMesquita. He found that bipolarity generally tended to be associated with more peaceful periods, supporting the notion that bipolarity is more likely to produce peace than war. "The greater the shift toward a multipolar system, the greater the amount of war that can be expected to begin during subsequent five years" (1975, 206). Note that he did not find that bipolar systems would always be equated with peace and stability, but only that multipolar systems would have more wars. This may be compared to Haas's findings that bipolar systems would have fewer wars, but that they would be prolonged and localized.

In terms of the types of data used in these studies, the Vietnam War represents only one observation. But given these findings, it is of more than passing interest that the Vietnam War exhibited several interesting characteristics. It was a localized war, but it did spill over into two adjacent countries, namely Cambodia and Laos. It was also a relatively long war; in terms of American involvement, it lasted from 1961 to 1973. But even considering only the active American involvement from 1965 to 1973, those eight years of war just about fit the average found in the Correlates of War project of 7.9 years (standard deviation of 19.3), and 7.6 years found by Levy for a longer time period (standard deviation of 16.9). However, if considered as an internationalized civil war beginning in 1961, when American casualties were first recorded, then the war lasted twelve years, somewhat longer than the average. It is interesting, therefore, that the configuration of the Vietnam War—given the empirical findings referred to above—is in some ways not particularly surprising, for it is the kind of war we might expect during the type of bipolar system existent throughout the 1950s and into much of the 1960s.

Finally, the world system approach takes the view that the world can be considered a complex system and can be seen as changing in regular patterns over very long periods of time. A number of components make up this system. One is the notion of "core" and "periphery" countries: at certain times one or more countries occupy what is called the core position and others are the peripheral countries. But these standings change, for a variety of reasons that are of little interest here. A second component is the idea that the relations between these two groups of countries, and other countries in the system, proceed through "long cycles," which can last up to two, three, or perhaps four hundred years. These relationships between core and periphery countries are thought to affect the overall types and patterns of international behavior in the world system.

In terms of wars and their relation to the long cycle of the world system, George Modelski has proposed that it may not be possible to predict the frequency or magnitude of war from these notions of the long cycle, but it may be possible to "demonstrate that the *character*—or type—of wars is in part determined by the nature of their global setting" (1979, 7). Thus, he suggests that "global" wars would be more common in periods when the world power preponderance is ambiguous. Systems of predominance (associated with a unipolar structure of world politics) would more likely have police actions. When the preponderance of the major world power is waning, nationalist wars would be more likely. "We would expect these wars to be relatively more likely in the latter phases of the long cycle of world politics, when the global system is moving toward multipolarity and losing its capacity for maintaining order, possibly in part because of the strain occasioned by the police actions of an earlier phase" (1979, 5-6).

In terms of the possibility of a patterned sequence in the occurrence of different types of war, Modelski, Johnson, and Wu suggest one pattern: global wars should be followed by police actions, followed by nationalist wars, and then regional and local disorders, which in turn should be followed by a period of global war. "Thus, during phases of low capability concentration or multipolarity, wars are likely to be global ones, while they are more likely to be police actions or nationalist wars in times, respectively, of high or falling concentration. Long cycle theory—and the disaggregation of war types it allows—may offer a new, possibly more comprehensive understanding of this complex issue" (1979, 7-8).

There seems little doubt that the post–World War II era was dominated by and large by the United States and the Soviet Union. The concentration of power was fairly high early in that era, with the United States the predominant power. Police actions occurred, such as the United States in Korea, several Latin American countries, and the Middle East, and the Soviet Union in its Eastern European client states. As power began to disperse, nationalist wars became more prominent. Most scholars consider the Vietnam War to be nationalist in nature, with the Vietnamese trying to break away, first from the French and then from the United States. It is plausible, therefore, that the type of war that involved the United States in Vietnam was to some extent a function of where the world system was in the 1950s and 1960s in terms of the long cycle.

CONCLUSION

This chapter has been aggregated and in some respects speculative. Focusing on the factors we have isolated in this chapter is risky in terms of what we might learn about the Vietnam War. Despite these risks, we have used these factors to look at the Vietnam War for two reasons: (1) in order to see the specifics of the war within the largest possible context, placing it within ongoing patterns and structures in the international system; (2) in order to link broadly gauged theory—whether concerning cyclicality of war or the effect of international system structure on national-scale behavior—to a specific case. While no direct, causal link can be drawn between any of these large-scale factors and the Vietnam War, nonetheless that war, as with all international events, took place within numerous large-scale contexts. To ignore the relationship between the latter and former might in fact impact on the limited ability of social scientists to provide policy advice, based on their studies of many cases, to a specific case.

It is of note that while the Vietnam War does in fact appear to fit into some long-term patterns, it did not produce what we would have expected in the smaller dimension of United States-Soviet relations. Since the war was widely justified as a result of the containment policy against international Communism, we would have expected United States-Soviet (and perhaps United States-Chinese) relations to be adversely affected. Such was not the case. The empirical evidence presented in this chapter suggests that the war had little negative effect on the continuing move toward détente between the United States and both the Russians and the Chinese. This conclusion might in fact be some further evidence for one of the models explaining the Vietnam War set out in chapter 3, a suggestion that will be taken up in the next chapter.

6. The Lessons of Vietnam

What are the "lessons" of the tragedy of Vietnam? Narrow questions yield narrow lessons and our focus thus far has been purposely broad. We are certainly not in a position at this point to pinpoint lessons on the conflict or the American involvement in it. But we are capable of reflecting on what might perhaps be called some of the "myths" surrounding the war.

At a conference at the University of Southern California held in February 1982, one of the many questions addressed was whether the war had not unfolded simply from a "collective deception" by American leaders about our role in the world, and whether that was not responsible for the beginnings of the American involvement. Others wondered whether United States leaders' "contempt" for the South Vietnamese led to the "loss" of Vietnam (Arizona Daily *Star*, 9 Jan. 1983). These are relatively narrow questions and do not address the American involvement in the broadest possible contexts of American foreign policy. To remain focused on these narrow questions is, potentially, to limit the lessons to be drawn from a massive tragedy, and perpetuates the myth that if we had only tried harder, or if certain decision makers had not been involved, things would have turned out differently.

Another illustration of the same type of myth concerns much of the intellectual ferment about the American involvement in the Vietnam War, especially beginning in the late 1960s. It was held that America was a decadent society, a police state, that we were a "violent" society, and administration after administration lied, deceived, and escalated the war despite what the public, and especially the informed elite, favored in foreign affairs. As one analyst suggested, "if history has not vindicated all of these assumptions the myth persists that smart-thinking people were way ahead of the administration and of the G.I. who was in the maw of the conflict" (Newmark 1982).

In fact, there was widespread support for the war and such support was greatest among the wealthier and better educated (including, as we shall see, some later critics of the war, as well as the editorial writers of the *New York Times*). Yet fifteen years later, when presidential candidate Ronald Reagan called the Vietnam War a "noble cause," the statement "set off titters throughout America's better educated set" (Kagan 1982).

Such myths as these tend, unfortunately, to become part of the political "religion," much as have many myths concerning domestic economic problems that emerged in the 1970s and 1980s (Schwarz, 1983).

WHAT HAVE WE LEARNED?

What have we learned about America's involvement in the Vietnam War from the viewpoints presented in the preceding chapters? First, we have learned that throughout the early part of the Cold War, neither American presidents nor the American public viewed the Vietnam situation as a highly important one; for long periods of time it was a peripheral issue. Even after 1954 and the surrender of the French at Dien Bien Phu, Americans paid relatively little attention to Vietnam, and their interest was aroused only in those years when a crisis erupted. Vietnam did not come to dominate the national consciousness until 1964-65, after the very early decisions for a commitment to Vietnam had already been made.

The reasons justifying American involvement in the war, like the interest in the entire Vietnam situation for the

United States, also changed over time. With one exception, symbolic perceptions of the Vietnam War were relatively few until late 1964 and early 1965, when they began to increase. The symbols (freedom, justice, democracy, and so on) were always present in the speeches of the Presidents, but saw increased use as the war escalated. The commitment to such symbols had not been as steady as the decision makers later implied.

We have also found that some historical evidence supports the notion that decision makers in the 1950s and early 1960s, operating in the framework of the containment policy, were responding rationally to what they felt was a threat to the United States and the Western world by the Communist movement in Vietnam, but there is also substantial evidence that questions this interpretation of American involvement and lends support to another model of decision making. The incremental model argues that even in the area of foreign affairs, individuals may not always make decisions based on a rational assessment of long-term goals and appropriate means, but rather, uncertain about their goals, they make any decision, just to avoid appearing indecisive. We have seen that each successive administration had as one of its goals not combatting Communism, or fighting an international conspiracy, or defending the Western world, but rather winning the next election; any decision that would save the next election was chosen, without necessarily anticipating the long-term effect of those decisions on the overall United States foreign policy posture.

At the same time that this concern for the next election influenced decision makers' perceptions of the options available to them in Vietnam, the underlying mood of the American public was also favorable to foreign involvement. Thus, options that at other times might have seemed preposterous were in the 1960s consistent with what the decision makers thought might land themselves a victory in that next election.

Public opinion polls showed that the American public, for

the most part, supported the United States role in Vietnam during the mid-1960s and did not waver from that conviction until 1969 at the earliest, or, depending on the specific question asked, possibly into the early 1970s. Even more broadly conceived indices show that for the entire 1941-68 period the United States was in what can be characterized as an extroverted mood in terms of foreign affairs involvement. Perhaps the most intriguing of all the evidence presented on this subject in chapter 4 was the analysis of the presidential State of the Union addresses, which reflected the shifts in mood: around 1967 and 1968, despite the continuation of the Vietnam War, it became clear that presidential focus on foreign affairs had waned in the annual address; and with few exceptions, this indicator continued on the low side even into the early 1980s.

Finally, we found that in the context of the larger Cold War, Vietnam did not seem to have any effect whatsoever on the trend toward cooperation and détente between the United States and the Soviet Union that characterized the previous fifteen years, and that culminated in President Nixon's dual trips to China and the Soviet Union in 1972. Nor did the Vietnam War appear to have negatively altered the pattern of growing cooperation between East and West in Europe. In fact, after a new high of cooperation in the mid-1960s following the Cuban Missile Crisis, one might have expected, given the pattern of swings since 1948, that the late 1960s would have brought increased tension between the two superpowers, and that the Vietnam War would have been a part of and would have exacerbated those tensions. The very opposite was true. There was only a small, imperceptible change toward greater tension in Europe during that period.

This finding is even more surprising when one considers that the onset of the Vietnam War corresponded with a period in which, according to patterns of international violence spanning the past 200 years, we might have expected a surge of such violence to occur. While there is a great deal of dispute about the interpretation and policy implications of such data, nonetheless the rough patterns that several scholars found were continued in the form of the Vietnam War. But this increased violence in the localized area of Southeast Asia did not spill over into the domain of generalized diplomatic relations between the two major powers involved.

Expanding our scope even further, we have drawn on the research of scholars investigating the effect of the structure of the international system on the decisions leaders make, as well as the phenomenon of the world system and the theory of the long cycle, which suggests that at certain points along that long cycle, some types of wars are more likely to occur than others. Some evidence suggests that at certain points along the continuum of unipolarity to multipolarity (each signifying how many major actors or "poles" are in existence in the international system), there is likely to be either more or less war in the system, and that during the period of the occurrence of the Vietnam War, conditions along that continuum were in fact conducive to somewhat more war in the system. These large-scale structural conditions, therefore, cannot be totally ignored even when considering the one case of the Vietnam War.

Other scholars have suggested that as the ruling hegemon in the world system begins to decline in power, nationalist wars are more likely to break out. The Vietnam War may be a case in point. Although there is still much dispute in scholarly circles in the United States over the exact character of the Vietnam War, a large segment of the scholarly community considered the war a legitimate nationalist uprising against first the French and then the United States. The evidence from these many perspectives, therefore, place the Vietnam experience in a much broader historical context than seeing it merely as a function of incorrect or devious decision making.

VIETNAM AS ABERRATION

There still remains, however, that gnawing question: was the American involvement in the Vietnam War merely an aberration, something that most Americans recognize as a mistake, that will not likely be repeated soon? In so much of the discussion concerning the American involvement in the Vietnam War, there seems to be the very implicit and very subtle notion that if we could somehow replay the early 1960s those crucial decisions resulting in the further United States involvement would not be made. But that is hindsight evaluation, about as good as someone saying "If you put me back at the peak of the stock market in September of 1929, I'll sell!" Most people, however, did not sell.

The data presented in the preceding chapters suggest that we should not treat Vietnam merely as an isolated aberration in American history, a unique event that can now be forgotten. Nor should we explain America's involvement in that war simply in terms of a few decisions that "got out of hand." To restrict analysis in this way is to restrict the type and scope of implications that can be drawn from American involvement in the Vietnam War. The war and the decisions producing it took place within an unfolding dynamic containing several crucial factors in a way militating for further American involvement, and not against it, and it is unlikely that a replay, with the same factors involved, would radically alter the outcome.

What were those crucial factors? First, while Vietnam for many years was not an important issue, decision makers nonetheless perhaps unwittingly allowed it to become one of overriding concern once early decisions had been made for involvement. Second, the public favored the war and as those early decisions were being made, the public, and the leading decision makers, were still engrossed in their extroverted view of the world. The American involvement in Vietnam was justified as part of the larger, Cold War policy of Russian containment; even though, while that justification was used time and again, the Vietnam War itself had virtually no effect on that Cold War. Relations between the two major protagonists continued in the cooperative direction (with only one deviation) that had been underway for almost twenty years.

On a yet larger scale, international violence had decreased prior to the major escalations of the war, possibly setting the stage, in the broadest sense, for yet another increase in such international violence somewhere in the world. In addition, the relations between the major powers in the world had undergone change, the primary one being the beginning demise of the United States as the recognized hegemon; and there is some evidence that when a hegemon declines, nationalist wars like the one in Vietnam, rather than other types of wars, are more likely to break out. This in no way means that the United States, or whatever hegemon may have been in existence, was destined to become involved in such a war, but only that in terms of the type of war likely to break out at such a time, nationalist wars would rank high in probability.

In sum, American foreign policy of the Vietnam era was not something constructed entirely anew by completely independent decision makers, even if we define the Vietnam era as having begun with the fall of the French. That policy had to be constructed in the context of many ongoing, dynamic processes that, while not recognized at the time in a conscious, explicit way, were nonetheless having their effect on day-to-day and week-to-week decisions. This is not to argue for an overly deterministic view but only to suggest that decision makers do not operate in a vacuum, and that we should explicitly recognize some of the constraints under which they actually operated.

To expand on this question of determinism for a moment, several observations can be made. First, none of the factors here have been suggested as direct causal links with the American involvement in the Vietnam War. They have all been viewed as background factors contributing to a certain generalized United States foreign policy stance that was operationalized in the specifics of the Vietnam War. That is, the specifics of the Vietnam War did not have to happen as they did; the general pattern of United States' foreign policy during that period, however, should not be seen either as surprise or an aberration.

In addition, however, it would behoove those who criticize the approach taken here as being too deterministic to realize that one highly popular view of the causes of the Vietnam War contains questionable assumptions about the determinants of foreign policy. As we have noted throughout, many take the position that decision makers knew all along what they were doing, and, by implication, knowing what would happen, they could have forestalled the tragedy of Vietnam. As some have argued, those early decisions made in the Vietnam situation set the course of the American involvement in Vietnam. Gelb and Betts illustrate this argument. After noting that in April 1975, the Americans were thrown out of Saigon, they point out that "ten years before, the Marines had splashed ashore at Danang," and twenty years before, the last of the French troops

> had departed from the divided country, only to be followed by scores of American advisors and hundreds of millions of dollars in American aid. Twenty-five years before, as North Korean troops raced toward Seoul, President Truman had made the commitment that brought all those Americans to Vietnam.
>
> It was as if destiny had been suspended since that day in 1945 when French forces returned to Indochina to reclaim their colonies (1979, 347).

There can hardly be a more deterministic argument than the one that says President Harry Truman's decisions in 1950 caused all those later decisions bringing about the American involvement in the Vietnam War. And yet this is what Neil Sheehan says in his introduction to the *New York Times* edition of *The Pentagon Papers*, when he contends that one of the broad conclusions of *The Pentagon Papers'* analysts was "that the Truman Administration's decision to give military aid to France in her colonial war against the Communist-led Vietminh 'directly involved' the United States in Vietnam and 'set' the course of American involvement" (1971, xi). President Truman's decisions, however, as well as those made later, especially by Presidents Kennedy and Johnson, were all themselves made within the larger contextual forces of American foreign policy. While describing this phenomenon in a somewhat more convoluted way,

Richard Ashley, in analyzing relations between the United States, the Soviet Union, and China in the contemporary era, nonetheless takes the same position.

> Some people will surely object to the arguments advanced here on the grounds that they are all too deterministic, that they demean human freedom, that they reduce people to the status of cogs in machines. The objection raises a crucial point. The social determinism expressed in the tragic logic of the modern security problematique and represented in the general model assumes only that participants unquestioningly take themselves to be free and thus fail to acknowledge their long-run dependence upon their environments. It is this technical-rational hubris, an equation of freedom with power, that leads people to deny social determinism, ignore historical processes, disdain of exercising their communicative capacities in the quest for consensus, and crash headlong into limits that they do not foresee and cannot surmount. Determinism exists, in short, but determinism and autonomy are not joined in either-or relation. For statesmen, bureaucrats, entrepreneurs, factory workers, farmers, and scholars, determinism is an ever-present, inescapable fact of life. People stride toward autonomy when, upon recognizing this to be so, they set out to escape the limits of technical rationality—to exercise their capacities for knowledge and communication to the fullest (Ashley 1980, 288).

For decision makers, in other words, to ignore the long-term forces within which they are operating may frequently—and perhaps Vietnam is the most recent example—be courting disaster.

AFTER VIETNAM

The specifics of the Vietnam case are now behind us, but the preceding material has suggested that we must view the American involvement in the Vietnam War as part of a very complex, ongoing dynamic, and not, as many have done, as an aberrant mistake, one that was unfortunate and to be forgotten. But what about the continuing dynamic of American foreign policy? How do the factors outlined in the preceding chapters appear now, in the generation after the Vietnam War? First, even by the early 1970s, public attention had begun to turn to other, mostly domestic, issues. While the Vietnam issue did not disappear from the policy agenda, it began to take on very secondary and then tertiary importance. The figures presented in chapter 2 on presidential attention to Vietnam showed that as early as two years before the end of the active American involvement, Vietnam had receded into the background. We also saw in chapter 2 that the type of issues decision makers saw as important in Vietnam also changed; the highly charged symbolic content of presidential speeches on Vietnam peaked out in the third quarter of 1967 and went through a gradual decline through the next five years, although never quite reaching the low levels of the early 1960s.

But since Vietnam was fast receding as a specific issue, to evaluate the post-Vietnam era in the broadest sense along the symbolic attention dimension it might be more profitable to investigate the level of presidential symbolic rhetoric in terms of the United States' entire foreign policy posture, and to do so over a longer period of time. Has this posture undergone change, and if so, when, and where do we stand now?

Townsend Hoopes noted that Kennedy's inaugural address in 1961 "was to prove a harbinger of his steady efforts to dilute the moralistic tone of United States' foreign policy set by Dulles." The goal was to provide a "true" perspective from which to view the world, "through lenses less tinged with ideology, and (problems) could thus be approached with a greater reasonableness by both sides" (1967, 13). More recently, in the mid-1970s, using the same logic, one could have been concerned about the highly moralistic tone of President Carter's pronouncements about foreign affairs, especially his consistent references to "human rights." If noth-

Figure 23. Symbolic Rhetoric in State of the Union Addresses, 1950-1980

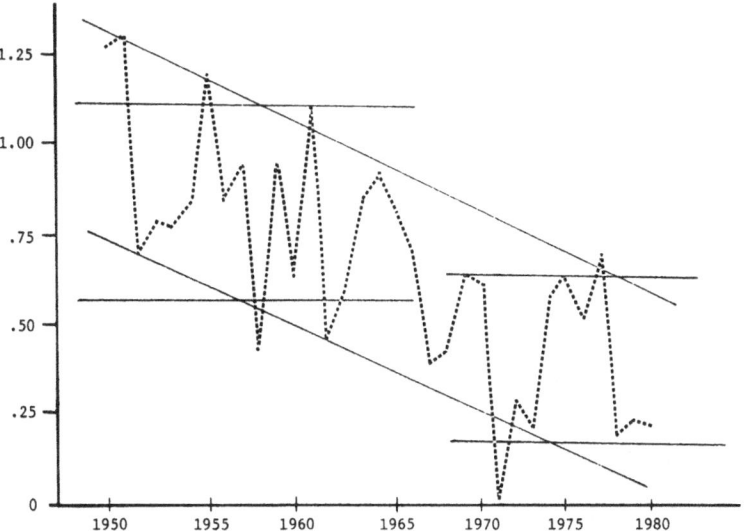

NOTE: Figure represents the number of symbols (see p. 35) per column-centimeter in the address as printed in *Papers of the President*. Symbols from President Nixon's 1971-1973 State of the World addresses are not included.

ing else, the attention given to this issue by observers reflected the concern that such moralistic issues may have signalled a shift in American foreign policy. These notions reflect the hypotheses set out in chapter 2 concerning the presence of such rhetoric and the overall foreign policy posture. Here we move beyond the Vietnam-related specifics and talk about foreign policy in general.

Using the same technique employed in chapter 2, we can track the presence of thirty-two symbols in State of the Union addresses from 1950 to the present, as displayed in figure 23 (symbols from President Nixon's 1971-73 State of the World addresses are not included). The number of symbols is controlled for the length of that part of the address devoted to foreign affairs. The data in figure 23 track fairly closely to the evidence presented in chapter 4 on attention devoted to foreign affairs as a whole. For one thing, there is an overall downward trend in the amount of symbolic content in the State of the Union addresses, as indicated in the banded section of the declining line. But within the general trend, several other things are of interest. First, 13 of the 19 years prior to 1966 had scores higher than 0.75; after 1966, not one year was above 0.75. Prior to 1966, only 1958 and 1961 scored below 0.50; after 1966, 5 out of 14 scored below 0.50 (or 8 if we count the three Nixon years of 1971-73). Thus, while there is an overall downward trend throughout the 31 years, there does also seem to be a step-level change beginning in the late 1960s, highlighted in the figure by the two sets of horizontal bands.

Second, this shift to a lower level of symbolic rhetoric in the State of the Union addresses was not a temporary phenomenon. To be sure, there was a slight upsurge between 1974 and 1977, but those years were no higher than the years 1969-70, and were roughly equal to the lowest years of the 1950s. From 1978 through 1980 we see some of the lowest scores in the entire thirty-year period. Even into the highly charged Reagan years, this measure of symbolic rhetoric remained extremely low relative to the previous thirty years. The symbolic content of the major foreign policy speech delivered annually by the president changed dramatically just about the time the overall attention devoted to foreign affairs decreased. The decreasing interest in foreign affairs corresponded with the decreasing use of symbolic terms to justify that interest. That same foreign policy posture continued into the 1980s.

Third, some of the specific shifts in figure 23 are also of interest. While Kennedy's first address in 1961 following Eisenhower's 1961 address was substantially lower in symbolic rhetoric, it increased in 1962 and 1963 (contrary to what Hoopes had suggested), as he became more involved in Vietnam. Johnson's level in 1964 was slightly higher still, but the addresses from 1965 to 1967, despite the increase in rhetoric in Vietnam addresses, actually decreased. Finally, despite Carter's extensive reliance on human rights as an issue, the Carter years show a clear drop from the Ford years, and Carter's speeches were drastically lower in symbolic rhetoric than almost all of the years from 1950 to 1970. (This finding would suggest that much of the popular perception of a president's foreign policy posture may not be supported by investigation of systematic evidence. One wonders, for instance, what we might conclude if we systematically investigated the popular charge that President Jimmy Carter was ineffective in foreign affairs.)

While there is an overall decline in rhetoric during the whole period, the years subsequent to 1966 indicate a shift from the earlier period. Not only did a structural shift occur at about the time Klingberg suggested it would in the overall introverted-extroverted pattern of American foreign policy moods, but this data also shows that the shift corresponded to an equally important shift in the type of words used by successive American presidents on America's foreign involvement. This most likely lasted even into the early 1980s, during the first four years of a Republican president pledged to restore the United States to its former greatness in foreign affairs. The step-level change that occurred in the late 1960s was not a short-lived phenomenon; it has had a continuing and obviously strong effect on the United States' view of itself in the world.

If we shift our level of analysis of American foreign policy to the process of decision making, we find that the postwar period has been characterized by what has come to be called the "Vietnam syndrome": every American move in foreign policy has been carefully scrutinized for its possible resemblance to Vietnam decision making. The American public has developed a fear of being "dragged into" a Vietnam-like quagmire. Even the popular novel *The Spike* suggested that such an outcome was on the minds of Soviet leaders during the Vietnam war itself; according to a fictional internal Directive,

> the war had produced a deep rift within the United States and had lent momentum to anti-American feeling

abroad. A growing body of Americans had come to accept that the war could not be won and that the best way out was through a negotiated settlement. "It is not in the Soviet interest," the Directive stated, "to assist a negotiated settlement at this stage." The reason was that the consciousness of American defeat, if permitted to grow, would be bound to produce domestic upheavals and eventually paralysis. Defeated in Vietnam, the United States would refuse to contemplate military intervention abroad for many years—opening up many opportunities for the progressive forces to expand their sphere of influence (deBorchgrave and Moss 1980, 65-66).

Moreover, the power of this Vietnam syndrome does not relate solely to American foreign policy. Many observers, while abhorring the Russian invasion of Afghanistan in 1979, nonetheless felt that an American response was unnecessary because of the high probability that Afghanistan would turn out to be "Russia's Vietnam." Such an outcome, it was hypothesized, would bring about the same result in the Soviet Union as in the United States: fear and reluctance about taking on any extensive foreign policy ventures because of the "Afghanistan syndrome."

This fear of yet another Vietnam-type involvement led scholars and former administration officials to scrutinize the process of decision making that led the United States into Vietnam, as if, once that process was laid out, it would not likely be repeated. We can attack this issue by citing several studies on the decision making during the Vietnam War. Leslie Gelb and James Betts, for instance, contend that the political system worked, that decision making on Vietnam was not an aberration from the normal process of foreign policymaking: "The political system did what a democratic system usually does: produce a policy responsive more to the majority and the center than to the minority or the extremes of opinion" (1979, 354).

Terry Nardin and Jeremy Slater, however, make the exact opposite argument in criticizing the Gelb and Betts work: "the war represented a breakdown of the democratic system, and the manner in which it was fought constituted a dramatic collapse of both reason and morality" (1981, 448). While in retrospect Nardin and Slater are correct in that morality and rationality did not take a front seat in American decisions on the Vietnam War, Gelb and Betts are also correct in that decisions were made in response, as was shown in chapter 4, to the majority. The first important point here is that democratic systems concerned with majority rule do not necessarily produce decisions that are the most in line with reason and morality, and part of the explanation for that is related to the decision-making model presented in chapter 3.

In fact, the presence of and strength of this Vietnam syndrome itself says something very important concerning the evaluation we give to each of the decision-making models presented in chapter 3. That is, in some ways there is implicit in this entire issue a subtle confirmation of the alternative to the rational model described in that chapter, the incremental or quicksand model. When it is argued that present United States policy moves (whether in the Middle East, Latin America, or elsewhere) may be getting the United States into another Vietnam, the contention is that we got bogged down in Vietnam through the process of incremental and quicksand decision making.

Almost every foreign adventure proposed by successive administrations since 1974 was viewed by the press, Congress, and the public as that possible first step into the bog, the beginning of a process, it is argued, that earlier turned out to be disastrous in Vietnam. Suggestions for further minor aid to Vietnam when the North Vietnamese were taking over in 1975 were strongly opposed by the public and Congress. Information that surfaced in 1976 about aid to one faction in Zaire resulted in strong public and Congressional opposition. In 1980, Secretary of State Cyrus Vance resigned in protest over President Jimmy Carter's use of force to rescue the American hostages being held by the Iranian government in Tehran because of his fear that the use of such force could slowly involve the United States directly in the Middle East. Zbigniew Brzezinski called Vance "the last Vietnam casualty." "Vance is so worried after the disastrous use of force in Vietnam that he lacks the will to use force again" (Arizona Daily *Star* 10 June 1980).

But Brzezinski was wrong, and showed his misunderstanding of contemporary American foreign policy. Vance was not the last Vietnam casualty. Perhaps nowhere did this Vietnam syndrome's effect on American foreign policy emerge more clearly than in the attempt by President Reagan in his early years in office to involve the United States by aiding the government of El Salvador and the antigovernment "contra" revolutionaries in Nicaragua (many of whom had been associated with the Somoza regime deposed by the Sandinistas in 1979), and by dispatching almost 2,000 United States Marines to Lebanon in 1983.

The administration portrayed the situation in Central America as a monstrous assault on the western hemisphere and more directly upon the security of the United States. Major white papers were produced, reminiscent of those the State Department produced during the Vietnam War. The situation in El Salvador was in some ways possibly more serious for the United States than Vietnam had ever been. It was geographically more proximate, for one thing, and strong evidence suggested that there was Cuban and possibly direct Soviet aid to the leftist rebels. The Sandinistas in neighboring Nicaragua had just successfully overthrown the Somoza government. Despite these facts, and despite the high praise and support the president was receiving at the time for his domestic economic programs, the public simply would not be budged when it came to El Salvador. The presence of fifty-five American advisors there in 1982 and 1983 was scrutinized openly and carefully, lest the ceiling be violated. The first American casualty in El Salvador, an American advisor killed in San Salvador in May of 1983, gained immediate front-page headlines throughout the United States. One opinion was overriding: minor decisions to send or increase aid could easily lead to another Vietnam process of decision making, and the public wanted nothing to do with it. This fear continued to exert a strong influence on the types of decisions that the foreign policy decision makers felt they could make, and the types of situations they could involve the nation in. Cyrus Vance, therefore, was only indicative of a strong underlying "Vietnam syndrome."

Lack of interest in such foreign policy ventures is interesting in light of the fact that, in the twelve months prior to the 1982 State of the Union address, the new administration had spent a great amount of time playing up the critical nature of the situation in El Salvador and its potential threat to the United States and to the western hemisphere. But Reagan's forceful stand on El Salvador proved to be a severe miscalculation, because the public was not budged. The administration read the response in a curious way. Aides to President Reagan proclaimed their sincerity in believing the seriousness of the situation, and that the administration was not simply looking for "a fight" or to enhance President Reagan's popularity by "playing on the national security theme." When polls showed the public turning against the administration's early moves in El Salvador, aides pointed to the press as the culprit, accusing it of playing El Salvador as another Vietnam. According to one aide, "when it became apparent that it was going to play that way, we had to low-key the issue." Said the aide: "What was wrong with El Salvador was the packaging of the activity, in terms of policy and presentation to the public. It wasn't well staged or sequenced" (Blumenthal, 1981).

A somewhat different response came from the administration concerning the United States Marines who had been dispatched to Lebanon to serve as part of the international peacekeeping force following the Israeli invasion of Lebanon in the summer of 1982. In that instance, even following the deaths of 236 Marines in the terrorist attack at the Beirut airport, the administration maintained its position: the Marines would stay. But news stories subsequent to the attack indicated that contingency plans were quickly being

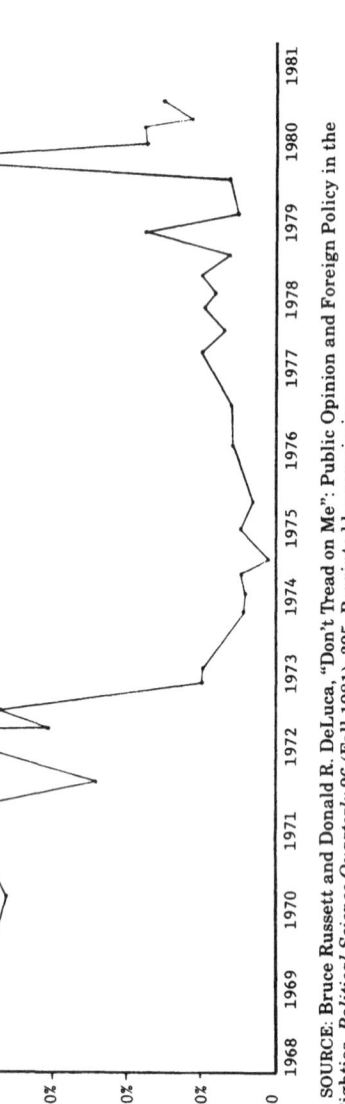

Figure 24. Respondents Choosing Foreign Affairs as Most Important Problem, 1968–1981

SOURCE: Bruce Russett and Donald R. DeLuca, "Don't Tread on Me": Public Opinion and Foreign Policy in the Eighties. *Political Science Quarterly* 96 (Fall 1981): 395. Reprinted by permission.

formulated to move the Marines back to the United States naval vessels off the coast of Lebanon. There was very strong opposition to the continuation of the Marines in Lebanon, both among the public and the Congress. Even major members of Congress, which in the fall of 1982 had given the president an eighteen-month extension for the Marine stay under the War Powers Act, were beginning to ask, by January of 1984, for a recall of the Marines. By early February, the administration, arguing that the Lebanese government was becoming more unstable and that the situation in Beirut was deteriorating, announced plans to withdraw the American Marines to the warships waiting off the Lebanese coast. Exiting with as much grace as possible, the Reagan administration contended that removing the Marines would actually enhance the situation in Lebanon. Alan Romberg, a State Department spokesman, said that the original deployment of the Marines had become an excuse for some of the warring factions to say, "We won't do anything until those people go," and that the objective of the removal of the Marines was "to make the multinational force more effective" (Arizona Daily *Star*, 9 Feb. 1984, 2).

In both instances the public and the Congress were exhibiting negative attitudes toward such foreign policy ventures. Cyrus Vance was clearly, therefore, not the "last of the Vietnam casualties." But to contend that the public is unreasonably introverted or apathetic about foreign affairs, or to contend that the mistake was one at the level of public relations is to ignore the entire context of American foreign policy in the early 1980s and its very important relationship to Vietnam. Not only had President Reagan devoted very little attention to foreign affairs in his first two years in office, but the public, despite its shift "toward a much more assertive, or hawkish, posture in world affairs" (Russett and DeLuca 1981, 382) was in no mood for long-term adventurism.

Figure 24 presents data on the percentage of those polled who chose foreign affairs as the most important issue facing the country (Russett and DeLuca 1981, 395), and shows that

Figure 25. Trends in Opinion about Defense Spending, 1960–1983

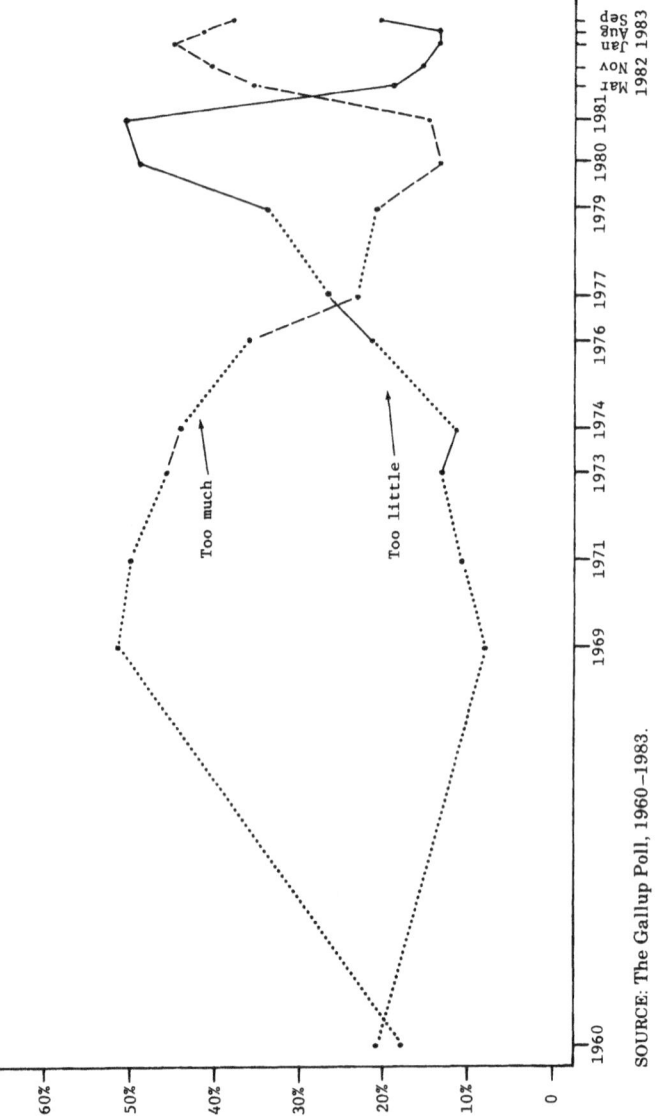

SOURCE: The Gallup Poll, 1960–1983.

the year 1980 was a clear aberration, a one-time reaction to two specific events. The year 1973 had represented a clear breakpoint, when the percentage feeling foreign affairs was the most important problem dropped from an average of roughly 36% between 1969 and 1972 to below 10%, and remained below 10% (except for one observation) until 1980. It then soared up to about 50%, not particularly surprising given the Iranian hostage situation and the invasion of Afghanistan in 1979. By 1981, however, the series shows a dramatic drop back down below 20%.

It would be fallacious to assume, however, that the post-Vietnam perceptions of American foreign involvement of the mid-1970s, perceptions reflecting basically the "Vietnam syndrome," will necessarily remain stable in the future any more than they did in the past. For one thing, attitudes toward the entire American defense posture are likely to change. For instance, the pattern in the responses to questions on United States' defense spending are instructive.

The period through the late 1950s and the early 1960s can be characterized as "hawkish," because the largest percentage of Americans thought too little was being spent on defense. By 1968 and 1969, however, an important crossover had definitely occurred, with a much larger percentage (50%) feeling that too much was being spent on defense compared to a mere 8% saying too little. This shift neatly coincides with the notion of a shift in mood to be taken up shortly. The point here is that public perceptions emerging in the 1970s that reflected an introverted mood must not be viewed as stable, and figure 25 indicates why. The eight years from 1968 to 1976 continually showed a higher percentage saying too much was being spent, but the differential was narrowing, and the crossover occurs once again in 1977-79. By 1980, a clear reversal had set in, with an average of about 53% feeling too little was being spent and roughly 10% feeling too much was being spent.

Seeing these trends, Russett and DeLuca concluded that "public opinion has again shifted, back toward a much more assertive, or hawkish, posture in world affairs, toward a widespread determination to rebuild American military capabilities and to reaffirm a readiness to use those capabilities in defense of perceived interests abroad" (1981, 382).

Russett and DeLuca may have been correct, but figure 25 also shows that for 1976-79 the figures ran roughly in tandem, and that the real shift occurs in 1980 (with a slight reversal in 1981). The question arises whether their conclusion, in its broad sweep, is correct, or whether this was only a short-term reaction to the capturing of the United States' citizens in Iran and the Russian invasion of Afghanistan in 1979. Russett and DeLuca in a sense agree: "Meanwhile, analysts should be impressed by how much they do not know about the causes or stability of foreign policy attitudes. It would seem foolhardy to make very firm predictions about whether present attitudes will remain constant for long" (1981, 199).

And that, of course is just the point: there is a consistency in foreign policy attitudes insofar as those attitudes, barring major international crises, take some time to change. A Gallup poll in 1981 showed that the percentages were almost the same as in 1980, with 51% feeling too little and 15% feeling too much was being spent on defense. But the astonishing fact is that by March of 1982 a Gallup poll showed that a major reversal toward basic dovishness had set in: 19% of those polled felt that too little was being spent on defense and 36% felt too much was in the defense budget (San Francisco *Chronicle* 1982, 2). There may be momentary shifts as in 1980, but lasting changes in those attitudes usually take a long time to materialize.

The evidence on the contemporary system is somewhat mixed, therefore. Foreign affairs was not viewed as the most important issue facing the country for the nine years 1973-81, with the one exception of 1980. After that one-year blip the figures returned to what they had been in the 1970s. Calls for increased defense spending have risen, but the data suggest a possible reversal may have been setting in by 1981.

The mood on the whole, therefore, still seems to be at

least moderately introverted. Even President Reagan, although promising a strong response to what he described as irregular Russian activities around the globe, registered only 18% devoted to foreign affairs in his 1982 State of the Union address, a particularly low score and one certainly in line with the low scores that had begun showing up in the late 1960s. In 1983, despite the many hot spots around the world and a new, and seemingly more bellicose Russian leadership, the president devoted only 22% of his State of the Union address to foreign affairs. In 1984 the amount devoted to foreign affairs increased slightly to 26%, but this was still very much in line with the lowest of scores registered in this most recent introverted era or any of the ones preceding it.

The argument up to this point has been that the United States, post-Vietnam, has exhibited a broadly based "Vietnam syndrome," which basically opposes foreign ventures. The empirical evidence suggests only a slight deviance from that. Analyzing the specific cases of attempted involvement in Central America as well as in Lebanon also suggests less than large-scale support. But Klingberg has made an interesting observation. Writing in 1979, and noting that during the last "consolidationist" period (1824 to 1871), the introvert phase lasted about twenty years and the extrovert about twenty-seven years, he contends that "the current introvert phase, which began to be fairly clear in 1966-1967 could then be expected to continue until 1986-1987, with the first sign of a shift towards extroversion apparent, say, by 1983" (Klingberg 1979, 43).

In addition to the aforementioned activities in Lebanon and Central America, the Reagan administration also undertook in the fall of 1983 a swift and surprising invasion of the small island of Grenada in the Caribbean, ostensibly because of the earlier takeover by a small Marxist group with supposed ties to Fidel Castro in Cuba. The public, by and large, supported the invasion. How does this square with the preceding argument? On the one hand, it would appear to contradict it, because it was a bellicose action reminiscent of extroverted eras in foreign policy; at the same time, it may have been nothing more than an aberrant case, not unlike the years 1979 and 1980 in the public opinion data analyzed above. In addition, there was no public debate. It was carried out secretly and swiftly, with most of the United States Marines leaving the island within weeks of the action. Had it been drawn out, had it begun to last several months, with casualties rising, the public's reaction might have been quite different. This is speculation, of course, but very plausible speculation.

Several months after the invasion of Grenada, an NBC news poll showed that, concerning economic, not military, aid to El Salvador, 52% of those polled were opposed to assistance and only 29% said they favored it. On the question of the Marines in Lebanon, the results were even more intriguing. Polled before the administration decision to remove the Marines to the warships offshore, 58% of those aware of the situation in Lebanon said that the troops should be brought home immediately, and only 36% said they should remain there until the president decided they should be brought home (Arizona Daily *Star*, 26 Jan. 1984, 10).

There seems little doubt, therefore, that public opinion on certain items, especially about defense spending, has shifted in the post-Vietnam era; and there have been certain actions, most notably in Lebanon and the invasion of Grenada, which would raise some doubts about this conclusion; but overall the public remained uninterested in pursuing strong foreign policy actions. The underlying mood reflected in these various sets of data has remained much the same, with some minor differences since the late 1960s, and can be seen as one major constraining force on the types of foreign policy decisions open to the United States' decision makers.

One point that should be made explicit now, that perhaps has only been implicit up to this point, is that all of this may not have been due solely to the existence of the specifics of the Vietnam War, but rather to the fact that longer-term processes were in operation, in which the Vietnam War was encapsulated, and brought about these changes. To act as if the mistake of Vietnam should not be allowed to interfere with realistic, moral, or rational American foreign policy is to fail to understand the broad dynamics in which that policy operates. It also therefore is a failure to see the possible paths along which that policy might fruitfully be directed, paths that would find the American public and Congress aligned with its leaders and their policies rather than opposed to them.

Three other factors can briefly be addressed concerning the post-Vietnam era, and these will of necessity be much more general because they are more large-scale, systemic, and aggregated factors than those already considered. We are therefore unable to measure them quite as easily, and inferences are more difficult to draw. But, for continuity and for reasons outlined many times already—their large-scale nature makes them no less important—we shall nonetheless give consideration to these systemic factors.

In terms of international structures, it became very clear throughout the Cold War years that the preeminence of the United States was waning. Whether we investigate defense expenditures as a single entity or other factors thought to measure the "power" of nations, the United States' major competitor—the Soviet Union—was closing the gap between the two nations (Sullivan, 1984). In addition to the increasing relative power of the Soviet Union over the United States, other power centers emerged, suggesting that the world was moving toward a more clearly multipolar rather than bipolar structure. China came onto the world scene with the announcement in the summer of 1971 by President Richard Nixon that he would visit the former enemy the following year. The year after that, in 1973, the Organization of Petroleum Exporting Countries startled the world community with sudden and drastic increases in world oil prices: Two more actors had to be contended with.

By the end of the American involvement in Vietnam, therefore, whether we place it at the end of active fighting in 1973 or the final ouster in 1975, the structure of the world power system had undergone radical changes. The world had become much more disarrayed than it had been at any time since World War II, and foreign policy much more difficult to construct and implement. Throughout most of his tenure in office Jimmy Carter faced the charges of incompetence, passivity, weakness, and impotence because he was not able to work his—or America's—wishes on the world.

The election of Ronald Reagan was to herald the dawn of a new era, but it didn't, and many of the same problems that haunted Carter also haunted Reagan. When he opposed the Soviet oil pipeline into Western Europe and tried to place embargoes on American companies doing business with the multinational consortium, he was quickly opposed by the Western Europeans and in short order backed down. In both Central America and the Middle East the President tried to exert influence with American aid, advisors, and troops. In Central America he was moderately successful, but it was also clear that a small group of Central American governments were also staking their claim for influence on the fighting in El Salvador, Nicaragua, and Guatemala. In the Middle East, after the dispatch of almost 2,000 American Marines, the loss of almost 250 of those Marines at the Beirut airport, and their redeployment to ships offshore, it was the Saudi Arabian government that in effect took over the task of trying to bring about peace among warring factions in Lebanon and between the Lebanese, the Syrians, and the Israelis, virtually ignoring the United States.

Of the obviously multiple reasons for these outcomes in United States foreign policies in the 1970s and 1980s, certainly one factor is the emergence of a much more multipolar world than had existed in the previous twenty years, and in such structures relationships between nations become more complex and unpredictable in that the international hierarchy is less stable and more equal.

Clearly what President Carter faced during his one term in office was still present in the international system during the first four years of the Reagan administration—a phe-

Lessons of Vietnam 177

nomenon that was new for the United States in the post–World War II era. In other words, other nations' foreign policy postures became—as the bipolar system was breaking down—more independent of the two major powers, and this of course applied as much to the Soviet Union as to the United States. What point the international political system has reached on the path from a bipolar to a multipolar system, and how many poles there are in the new system if we are already in a multipolar system, are questions very hard to assess. But we must recognize that the post-Vietnam era differs rather radically from the pre-Vietnam and Vietnam eras along this dimension, and this has already impacted upon United States foreign policy in the contemporary era.

When turning to the evidence on long-term violence in the international system, we noted (chapter 5) that while the evidence on the "cyclicality" or "periodicity" of war is contradictory, nonetheless many of the recent and more sophisticated analyses have suggested that strict periodicity does not exist. But nonetheless there were some suggestions that peaks and valleys do occur and follow one another. Singer and Small's up-dated data (1982, 150) show, for instance, that just about the time the total "nation-months of war underway" in the system reached the "0" point, it turned upward again, primarily as a result of the Vietnam War. With the end of that war, the series dips slightly and then increases again into 1980 at a higher level than reached during the Vietnam War years.

From about 1964 through 1980, therefore, the system witnessed—relative to the preceding ten years—an increased amount of system-wide war. This is confirmed even if one takes system size into account (figure 26, based on Singer and Small 1982, 151-54), although not quite as markedly. Given the large number of nations in the system after World War II, the amount of nation-months of war underway, controlling for system size, nowhere achieves the levels of the two World Wars or Korea. Nonetheless, an increase did occur. Moreover, the last four peaks—World War

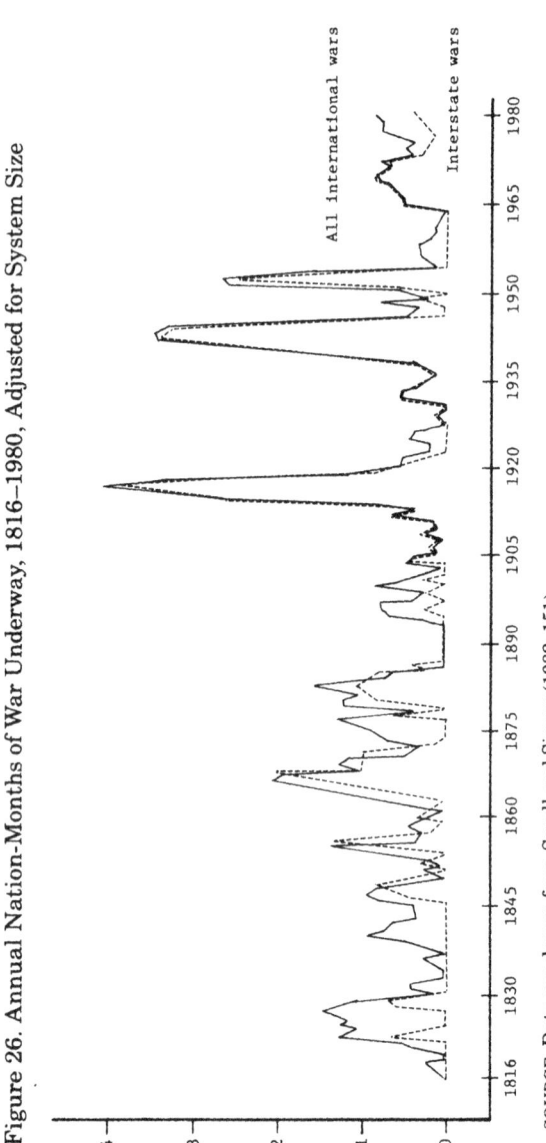

Figure 26. Annual Nation-Months of War Underway, 1816–1980, Adjusted for System Size

SOURCE: Data are drawn from Small and Singer (1982, 151).
NOTE: For international and interstate wars, see figure 22. Data are adjusted for the increase in the number of nations in the international system.

I, World War II, Korea, and the most recent era—were each successively lower. What can we expect now, in the post-Vietnam era, on this measure? Forecasting from this type of evidence is fraught with hazards, but one can certainly suggest that, using first only the total nation-months of war underway, without controlling for system size, the empirical evidence would suggest a diminution of war in the system, based on the past peaks shown in chapter 5 and assuming 1980, roughly, to be yet another peak. One might not come to that conclusion using the nation-months of war controlling for system size, however. Figure 26 shows, as noted, that the most recent peak is not nearly as marked as the previous three, and even pales when compared with earlier peaks. In addition, if one roughly estimates the number of years between the upsurges in violence in both streams of data, it works out to an average 16 years for all international wars (standard deviation = 5) and 15.4 years for interstate wars (standard deviation = 9). If we take 1964 as the year of the most recent upsurge, then 1980 does look suspiciously like the year signalling a new upsurge. It may very well be, therefore, that a post-1980 surge in nation-months of war might be underway (one certainly gains that impression from news accounts through 1979-1984). It could very well be that the wars between Russia and Afghanistan, Iran and Iraq, Israel and Lebanon, Chad and Libya, as well as others in the immediate post-1980 period are contributing to this upswing. But it is unlikely that such a surge would continue for very long, and certainly the United States involvement will be affected, as it probably already has been, in both Central America and the Middle East, by the "post-Vietnam syndrome."

CONCLUSION

This book has had several goals. The primary one was to show how the American involvement in the Vietnam War must be viewed not as a single, time-bound, isolated, aberrant incident, but as part of the dynamic of American foreign policy. To do this we have viewed the United States involvement in the war from the perspective of several different theoretical orientations, for to utilize only one of these would be to present a distorted and overly simplistic picture of American foreign policy and of the place of the Vietnam War in it, and therefore also to produce distorted, simplistic, and perhaps limited lessons concerning the Vietnam War.

American foreign policy after Vietnam flows at least partly from the context of that involvement: the war itself has had a dramatic effect on the United States' overall relationship to the outside world. American foreign policy is a dynamic entity, reacting both to events and situations in the outside world, but also to long-range domestic trends. Thus, the United States reverted during the 1970s to an extremely introverted mood, which continued into the 1980s, despite efforts by individual leaders to change that stance. That mood, however, will not remain static, and while it should last well into the 1980s and perhaps early 1990s, it will, if the historical record is of any help, shift again in the future. When change does occur, there is no way of forecasting what type of extroversion will occur, or in what form, or where.

Klingberg has made some tentative forecasts concerning these questions, but they are very general. He suggests, for instance, that some issues that might prompt a return of extroversion in United States foreign policy would be the Third World demand for a New International Economic Order, the search for justice and equality in Southern Africa and the danger of major hostilities there, the crisis in energy, the continuing crises in the Middle East, the arms race, the potential for further Communist influence in parts of the world, and, of course, "the possibility of a major military threat from the Soviet Union or China, or from a Sino-Soviet war" (1979, 45-46).

The point, Klingberg argues, is that the United States "should be preparing for special world crises and challenges in the late 1980s," and suggests that, after 1986, and depending on the nature of the challenges, the United States could be expected to emphasize either a military response to these challenges; or, and in his judgement more likely, "to exercise political, economic, cultural, and moral leadership, thereby attracting wide world support and cooperation in building a more just and stable international order stressing human respect, freedom and human concern" (1979, 49). It is, as noted above, extremely difficult to forecast in any specific fashion what types of extroverted actions might be utilized. But the important point is that the mood is susceptible to change; it is dynamic. Moreover, we have tried to show that such moods are amenable to tracking for possible evidence of upcoming shifts.

But these changes in domestic perceptions of the role of the United States in the world will take place within the context of larger, long-term changes taking place within the broader context of international politics. Whether we are to focus on various types of international structures describing the makeup of the international system or the shifts in the amount of violence in international politics, the point is that all of these are going to impact, over the long term, on the types of decisions United States' foreign policy decision makers will be in a position to make. These are large scale, long-term, and highly aggregated types of phenomena— which means they are very easy to ignore in concern about day-to-day diplomatic events—but that makes them no less important.

Within these larger contours of shifting moods and international structures resides the somewhat more specific relationship between the two superpowers. Since 1946, United States-Soviet relations have alternated between détente and nondétente periods. Thus it is fallacious to view the Cold War as having ended somewhere around the late 1960s, and the Nixon years as having ushered in détente. Evidence presented in chapter 5 suggests that there has been a roughly linear trend toward more cooperative relations, and that the Nixon years were in fact a culmination of this twenty-year trend. Beyond the early 1970s, we find once again a period of relative breakdown in détente; in figure 22, 1975 can be seen as the beginning of the end of détente between the United States and the Soviet Union. Starting in 1976, relations soured again, reaching levels of conflict found in earlier years of the Korean War, the Soviet shooting down of the American U-2 in 1960, and the United States' military buildup in Vietnam. By 1977 both the United States and the Soviet Union relied on the time-tested technique of ejecting each other's newspaper reporters as diplomatic signals of dissatisfaction. Those difficulties may of course have been laying the groundwork for another détente period, which would confirm the existence of an ever-changing, fluctuating pattern of both American foreign policy and American-Soviet relations.

Hopes for long-term peace after World War II were dashed, first by the Korean War and later by the American involvement in Vietnam. After that involvement ended, the hope emerged that in the modern era of destructive weapons, war had come to an end and that the Vietnam War was America's last. But the involvement in Vietnam illustrated the potential futility of resting one's hopes on such a chimera, for it suggested once again that international violence may continue, as it has in the past, to plague mankind. This does not mean that the United States would be a necessary participant in any future violence, but certainly as Vietnam recedes into history, foreign policy decision makers should become more alert to the escalatory potential of crisis situations or confrontations involving the United States.

The strong emotions and ideological heat generated by the Vietnam War were quickly replaced by a mood of quiescence about American foreign policy. Because the war had been a costly failure, there seemed to develop a groupthink perception of it as an unseemly aberration. Thus, the very immediate, recent experience of the war itself served as a jumping-off point for perceptions of future American foreign policy. But policy formulated through a focus on the immediate past events of history is parochial policy, without benefit of the larger historical contexts or configurations in which any specific issue emerges and must be considered.

One would be mindful to recall the learned economists who met to debate the question, "Is the Business Cycle Obsolete?" in 1967, after the long economic expansion of the 1960s. One year after the conference proceedings were published, in 1969, the American economy was in a recession. But even then, optimists held to the view that economic expansion "could (still) be taken as the norm" (Klein 1976, 2). Four years later came the wracking recession of 1973-74. Remarked Klein: "We should have learned in the 1960s to be wary when the change is supported by data which may cover only the most recent past and which may therefore represent ephemeral conditions" (1976, 18).

Holsti and Rosenau, who have extensively investigated public opinion in the post-Vietnam era, agree, although for slightly different reasons based on their evidence:

> In the absence of dramatic or traumatic unifying episodes—for example, another Pearl Harbor—policy legitimacy may prove to be an elusive goal for the near term. To the extent that this prognosis is valid it suggests that bold American undertakings aimed at achieving fundamental changes in the international system are likely to trigger long and divisive domestic debates.... Even the anticipation of such confrontations is likely to be an important constraint on the conduct of American foreign policy (Holsti and Rosenau 1980, 297).

These authors go on to remark, however, writing in 1980, that the then-as-yet-unresolved hostage crisis in Iran or the Soviet invasion of Afghanistan might prove to be just such a catalyst "for creation of a new foreign policy consensus in this country, much as the attack on Pearl Harbor was almost four decades ago" (1980, 297). Now, of course, with hindsight, we know that neither of these events provided such a catalyst. The evidence presented at several points already in this and earlier chapters concerning the American involvement in both Central America, the Caribbean, and the Middle East would suggest that none of these "hot spots"— at least to date—provided such a catalyst either.

All of this would tend to confirm the strength of long-term forces. Unfortunately, the longer an era lasts, in some ways, the more complacent one becomes. Thus, while the Reagan administration did run into massive opposition to its foreign policy positions from Americans who still remembered the Vietnam experience, evidence presented earlier in this chapter does suggest that some of those constraints may be breaking down; although the process itself will take many years, and we cannot forecast in which way perceptions of future American policy should go.

Post-Vietnam foreign policy cannot be constructed either as if the Vietnam War had never happened, or as if it was merely a mistake. The present situation of the United States in the world, and the policies being formulated to react to that situation, are strongly constrained, and will themselves constrain and move future foreign policy leaders in certain directions.

None of what has been said here can in any way exonerate foreign policy decision makers. Incorrect and bad decisions were made; there were certainly attempts at several junctures to mislead, or at least withhold, information from the public and the press as well as from Congress. For years, especially beginning with President Kennedy, decision makers did not make the decisions they might have made to transform the involvement into something more positive, or to extricate the United States earlier, or both. Just as the perspectives utilized here do not imply that decision makers were free of responsibility, likewise they do not mean that the events that happened in the United States' involvement in Vietnam in some way had to happen.

Yet those events did happen, and to fail to recognize a gross mistake or to treat it as nothing more than a mistake that will of course not be repeated again can only contribute to future mistakes. But just as no decision makers can be exonerated for their decisions on Vietnam, it is equally fallacious to disregard the entire venture solely as a function of either evil or incorrect decisions, with the implication that had other decision makers been in charge, better decisions would have been made.

The popularity of David Halberstam's book on Vietnam, *The Best and the Brightest*, in an indirect way attests to the popularity of the rationalized, calculating model of decision making in Vietnam. Halberstam's book implies first that even the best and the brightest managed to botch things up horribly. Second, and more broadly, Halberstam suggests that the pattern of American decisions in the Vietnam War can somehow be traced back to the personality makeup and individual goals and values of the individual leaders. The series of vignettes of the individuals involved in Vietnam that constitute most of the book subtly link those individuals to the decisions—bad ones—that were made in Vietnam. Although not saying it in so many words, Halberstam is highly critical of those decision makers.

The Best and the Brightest was actually Halberstam's second book on Vietnam. After covering the war as probably one of the most successful and effective American correspondents in Vietnam in the early 1960s, Halberstam wrote *The Making of a Quagmire*, published in 1965. Jude Wanniski, in a telling review of *The Best and the Brightest* in the *Wall Street Journal*, observed that in the wake of Ngo Dinh Diem's death in Vietnam in 1963, when Lyndon Johnson and his advisors were trying to decide whether to take over or walk away, "they were breathing the same air as David Halberstam was, weighing the same risks and options against the same political backdrop of the moment" (1972, 26). At that time, Halberstam, reflecting the "historical imperative," actually strongly favored America's further involvement.

What about withdrawal? Few Americans who have served in Vietnam can stomach this idea. It means that those Vietnamese who committed themselves fully to the United States will suffer the most under a Communist government, while we lucky few with blue passports withdraw unharmed; it means a drab, lifeless and controlled society for a people who deserve better. Withdrawal also means that the United States' prestige will be lowered throughout the world, and it means that the pressure of Communism on the rest of Southeast Asia will intensify. Lastly, withdrawal means that throughout the world the enemies of the West will be encouraged to try insurgencies like the one in Vietnam. Just as our commitment in Korea in 1950 has served to discourage overt Communist border crossings ever since, an anti-Communist victory in Vietnam would serve to discourage so-called wars of liberation (1965, 315).

Hindsight criticism of those whose decisions escalated American participation in Vietnam in the mid-1960s is easy to come by. When we look at the evidence, however, we find that it was not only the leading decision makers at the time, but the public as well as many later critics who by and large supported the general drift of American foreign policy at the time, a drift that included further involvement in the Vietnam War.

The warp and woof of American foreign policy is a densely complex dynamic. To the extent policymakers fail to place themselves, their nations, and their policies within historical perspectives such as those proposed here, they will fall victim to myopia, failing to realize that the issues, problems, and situations they find themselves in cannot be solved on an ad hoc basis. Understanding how a situation has evolved may often be as important to solving it as understanding the specifics of the issue itself. Foreign policies cannot be created on an ad hoc basis, in a *tabula rasa* fashion.

This is more than simply reiterating the simplistic notion that history repeats itself, or that we are doomed to repeat history if we do not study it. History does not repeat itself, at least in a purely mechanistic way; but nonetheless, there are patterns in the fluctuations of the historical process— and what we have set out here are some of the factors that can be used to analyze historical situations within some contexts and to compare them with previous situations.

References

Agency for International Development, Office of Statistics and Reports, Bureau for Program and Policy Coordination. U.S. Overseas Loans and Grants, and Assistance from International Organizations. Special Report Prepared for the House Foreign Affairs Committee, May 14, 1971.

Allison, Graham. 1971. *Essence of Decision: Explaining the Cuban Missile Crisis.* Boston: Little, Brown.

Arizona Daily *Star,* 10 June 1980; 9 Jan. 1983; 26 Jan. 1984; 9 Feb. 1984.

Arizona Daily Wildcat. 29 July 1980, p. 15.

Ashley, Richard K. 1980. *The Political Economy of War and Peace: The Sino-Soviet-American Triangle and the Modern Security Problematique.* London: Frances Pinter Ltd.

Azar, Edward. 1973. *Probe for Peace: Small State Hostilities.* Minneapolis: Burgess.

Azar, Edward, and Thomas J. Sloan. 1975. *Dimensions of Interaction: A Source Book for the Study of Behavior of 31 Nations from 1948 to 1973.* Occasional Paper no. 8. International Studies Association. Pittsburgh: University of Pittsburgh Center for International Studies.

Azar, Edward E., Richard A. Brody, and Charles A. McClelland. 1972. *International Events Interaction Analysis: Some Research Considerations.* Beverly Hills: Sage.

Berman, Larry. 1982. *Planning a Tragedy: The Americanization of the War in Vietnam.* New York: W.W. Norton.

Blumenthal, Sidney. Marketing the President. *New York Times Magazine* September 13, 1981.

Bodard, Lucien. 1967. *The Quicksand War.* Boston: Little, Brown.

Britannica Book of the Year. London: The Encyclopedia Britannica Co., Ltd., 1950-1970.

Bueno deMesquita, Bruce. 1975. Measuring Systemic Polarity. *Journal of Conflict Resolution* 19 (June): 187-16.
Burgess, Philip M., and Raymond W. Lawton. 1972. *Indicators of International Behavior: An Assessment of Events Data Research.* Beverly Hills: Sage.
Caspary, William R. 1972. The "Mood Theory": A Study of Public Opinion and Foreign Policy. In *Political Attitudes and Public Opinion*, ed. Dan D. Nimmo and Charles M. Bonjean, 439-54. New York: David McKay.
Chester, Lewis, Godfrey Hodgson, and Bruce Page. 1969. *An American Melodrama: The Presidential Campaign of 1968.* New York: Viking Press.
deBorchgrave, Arnaud, and Robert Moss. 1980. *The Spike.* New York: Avon Books.
Denton, Frank H., and Warren Phillips. 1968. Some Patterns in the History of Violence. *Journal of Conflict Resolution* 12 (June): 182-95.
Department of Defense OASD (Comptroller), Directorate for Information Operations. *Statistics on Southeast Asia.* April 18, 1973.
Draper, Theoodore. 1967. *The Abuse of Power.* New York: Viking Press.
Edelman, Murray. 1964. *The Symbolic Uses of Politics.* Urbana: Univ. of Illinois Press.
———. 1971. *Politics as Symbolic Action: Mass Arousal and Quiescence.* New York: Academic Press.
Eidenberg, Eugene. 1969. The Presidency: Americanizing the War in Vietnam. In *American Political Institutions and Public Policy*, ed. Allan P. Sindler, Boston: Little, Brown.
Ellsberg, Daniel. 1970. Escalating in a Quagmire. Paper delivered at the 66th annual meeting of the American Political Science Association, September, Los Angeles.
———. 1972. *Papers on the War.* New York: Simon and Schuster.
Gallucci, Robert L. 1975. *Neither Peace nor Honor: The Politics of American Military Policy in Vietnam.* Baltimore: Johns Hopkins Univ. Press.
Gelb, Leslie. 1970. Vietnam: Some Hypotheses About How and Why. Paper delivered at the 66th Annual Meeting of the American Political Science Association, September, Los Angeles.
——— and Richard K. Betts. 1979. *The Irony of Vietnam: The System Worked.* Washington: Brookings Institution.
George, Alexander, et al. 1971. *The Limits of Coercive Diplomacy: Laos, Cuba, and Vietnam.* Boston: Little, Brown.

Geyelin, Philip. February 4, 1982, p. 18. Did Vietnam Statistics Lie? *Sacramento Bee.*
Goldmann, Kjell. 1973. East-West Tension in Europe, 1946-1970: A Conceptual Analysis and a Quantitative Description. *World Politics* 26 (October): 106-125.
Goodwin, Richard. 1966. *Vietnam: Triumph or Tragedy?* New York: Random House.
Graff, Henry F. 1970. *The Tuesday Cabinet: Deliberations and Decisions on Peace and War under Lyndon Johnson.* Englewood Cliffs, N.J.: Prentice-Hall.
Haas, Michael. 1970. International subsystems: Stability and polarity. *American Political Science Review* 64 (March): 98–123.
———. 1974. *International Conflict.* Indianapolis: Bobbs-Merrill.
Halberstam, David. 1969. *The Best and the Brightest.* New York: Random House.
———. 1965. *The Making of a Quagmire.* New York: Random.
———. 1971. The Programming of Robert McNamara. *Harpers,* Feb., 56-74.
———. 1968. *The Unfinished Odyssey of Robert Kennedy.* New York: Random House.
Hilsman, Roger. 1967. *To Move a Nation.* New York: Dell.
Holmes, Jack E. 1977. American Foreign Policy Regarding Six Geographic Regions. Paper delivered at the 18th Annual Convention, International Studies Association, 17 Mar., St. Louis.
Holsti, K. 1966. Resolving International Conflicts. *Journal of Conflict Resolution* 10 (September): 272-96.
Holsti, Ole R. and James N. Rosenau. 1980. Cold War Axioms in the Post-Vietnam Era. In *Change in the International System,* ed. Ole R. Holsti, Randolph M. Siverson, and Alexander L. George. Boulder, Col.: Westview Press.
Hoopes, Townsend. 1967. *The Limits of Intervention.* New York: David McKay.
Howell, Llewellyn D. 1983. A Comparative Study of the WEIS and COPDAB Data Sets. *International Studies Quarterly.* 27: 149-159.
Hunter, Robert E. 1972-1973. Power and Peace. *Foreign Policy* 9: 37-54.
Janis, Irving L. 1972. *Victims of Groupthink: A Psychological Study of Foreign Policy Decisions and Fiascoes.* Boston: Houghton Mifflin.
Kagan, Robert W. April 1, 1982. Realities and Myths of the Vietnam War. *Wall Street Journal.* p. 29.

Katz, Daniel. 1967. Group Processes and Social Integration: A System Analysis of Two Movements of Social Protest. *Journal of Social Issues* 23:3-22.

Kegley, Charles W., and Eugene R. Wittkopf. 1981. *World Politics: Trend and Transformation.* New York: St. Martin's.

Kiessler, Charles A. 1971. *The Psychology of Commitment: Experiments Linking Behavior to Belief.* New York: Academic Press.

Kissinger, Henry. 1969. *American Foreign Policy.* 143 pp.

Klein, Philip A. 1976. *Business Cycles in the Postwar World: Some Reflections on Recent Research.* Washington, D.C.: American Enterprise Institute.

Klingberg, Frank L. 1952. The Historical Alternation of Moods in American Foreign Policy. *World Politics* 4 (Jan.): 239-73.

———. 1979. Cyclical Trends in American Foreign Policy Moods and Their Policy Implications. *Challenges to America: United States Foreign Policy in the 1980s.* Ed. Charles W. Kegley, Jr., and Patrick J. McGowan. Beverly Hills: Sage.

Lasswell, Harold D., Nathan Leites, and associates. 1968. *Language of Politics: Studies in Quantitative Semantics.* Cambridge: MIT Press.

Laurence, Edward J. 1976. The Changing Role of Congress in Defense Policymaking. *Journal of Conflict Resolution* 20 (June) 213-54.

Levi, Werner. 1970. Ideology, Interests, and Foreign Policy. *International Studies Quarterly* 14 (March): 1-31.

———. 1981. *The Coming End of War.* Beverly Hills: Sage.

Levy, Jack S. 1981. Alliance and War Among the Great Powers. *Journal of Conflict Resolution* 25 (December): 581-613.

———. 1983. *War in the Modern Great Power System, 1495-1975.* Lexington: University Press of Kentucky.

Lindblom, Charles E. 1959. The Science of Muddling Through. *Public Administration Review.* 19 (Spring): 79-88.

Lunch, William M., and Peter W. Sperlich. 1979. American Public Opinion and the War in Vietnam. *Western Political Quarterly* 32 (March): 21-44.

McClelland, Charles D. 1983. Let the User Beware. *International Studies Quarterly* 27 (June): 169-178.

McGowan, Patrick J.; and Robert M. Rood. 1975. Alliance Behavior in Balance of Power Systems: Applying a Poisson Model to Nineteenth-Century Europe. *American Political Science Review* 69 (September) 859-70.

Miller, Lawrence W., and Lee Sigelman. n.d. Continual Nibbling or a Good Bite? The Johnson Vietnam Policy, 1967-1969. Department of Political Science, Texas Tech University. Mimeo.
Mitchell, Joyce M., and William C. Mitchell. 1969. *Political Analysis and Public Policy: An Introduction to Political Science*. Chicago: Rand McNally.
Modelski, George. 1974. *World Power Concentrations: Typology, Data, Explanatory Framework*. Morristown, NJ: General Learning Press.
Modelski, George; Richard Johnston; and Friedrich W. Wu. 1979. The Long Cycle and Wars, 1770-1975: A Preliminary Test of Theory. Paper delivered at the annual convention, International Studies Association/West, and Western Political Science Association, Portland, Oregon, March 22-24.
Morse, Edward L. 1976. *Modernization and the Transformation of International Relations*. New York: Free Press.
Mueller, John E. 1973. *War, Presidents, and Public Opinion*. New York: John Wiley and Sons.
Nacht, Michael. 1980. The war in Vietnam: The Influence of Concepts on Policy. ACIS Working Paper No. 26. Los Angeles: Center for International and Strategic Affairs, University of California, July.
Nardin, Terry, and Jerome Slater. 1981. Vietnam Revised. *World Politics* 33 (April):436-48.
Newmark, Todd L. 1982. A Parade Won't Heal the Divisions Over Vietnam. *Wall Street Journal*, November 10, p. 29.
Newsweek. 12 June, 1972, p. 78. Know Your Enemy.
Pfeiffer, Richard M. 1968. *No More Vietnams?* New York: Harper and Row.
Pool, Ithiel deSola. 1970. *The Prestige Papers: A Comparative Study of Political Symbols*. Cambridge: MIT Press.
Public Papers of the Presidents of the United States. (Washington, D.C.: United States Government Printing Office, 1945-1974). GS 4.113: 950-74.
Rapaport, Anatol. 1966. Strategic and Non-strategic Approaches to Peace. In *Strategic Interaction and Conflict*, ed. K. Archibald. Berkeley: Institute for International Studies.
Ravenal, Earl C. 1978. *Never Again: Learning from America's Foreign Policy Failures*. Philadelphia: Temple Univ. Press.
Roberts, Chalmers M. 1954. The Day We Didn't Go To War. *The Reporter* 11 (September 14), 31-35.

Rosenau, James. 1966. Pre-Theories and Theories of Foreign Policy. In *Approaches to Comparative and International Politics*, ed. R. Barry Farrell. Evanston: Northwestern Univ. Press.

Roskin, Michael. 1974. From Pearl Harbor to Vietnam: Shifting Generational Paradigms and Foreign Policy. *Political Science Quarterly* 89 (Fall):563-88.

Russett, Bruce, and Donald R. DeLuca. 1981. "Don't Tread on Me": Public Opinion and Foreign Policy in the Eighties. *Political Science Quarterly* 96 (Fall):381-400.

San Francisco *Chronicle*, April 6, 1982, "U.S. Public Thinks Russia Is Stronger," by George Gallup.

Schoenbrun, David. 1968. *Vietnam: How We Got In; How to Get Out*. New York: Atheneum.

Schwarz, John. 1983. *America's Hidden Success: A Reassessment of Twenty Years of Public Policy*. New York: W.W. Norton.

Schell, Jonathan. 1975. Reflections: The Time of Illusion; VI: Credibility. *New Yorker*, 7 July.

Scott, Peter Dale. 1970. Tonkin Bay: Was There a Conspiracy? *New York Review of Books*, 29 Jan. 1970.

Sheehan, Neil. 1971. *The Pentagon Papers*. New York: Bantam.

Simon, Herbert A. 1957. *Models of Man*. New York: Wiley.

Singer, J. David, and Melvin Small. 1968. Alliance Aggregation and the Onset of War, 1815-1965. In *Quantitative International Politics: Insights and Evidence*, ed. J. David Singer. New York: Free Press.

―――. 1972. *The Wages of War, 1816-1965: A Statistical Handbook*. New York: John Wiley and Sons.

Small, Melvin, and J. David Singer. 1979. Conflict in the International System, 1816-1977: Historical Trends and Policy Futures. In *Challenges to America: United States Foreign Policy in the 1980s*, ed. Charles W. Kegley and Patrick J. McGowan, 89-116. Beverly Hills: Sage.

―――. 1982. *Resort to Arms: International and Civil Wars, 1816–1980*. Beverly Hills: Sage.

Spitzer, Robert J. 1979. The President and Public Policy: A Preliminary Inquiry. *Presidential Studies Quarterly* 9 (Fall):441-56.

Sullivan, Michael P. 1972a. Commitment and the Escalation of Conflicts. *Western Political Quarterly* 25 (March):23-38.

―――. 1972b. Symbolic Commitment as a Correlate of escalation: The Vietnam case. In *Peace, War, and Numbers*, ed. Bruce Russett, Beverly Hills: Sage.

―――. 1974. Vietnam: Calculation or Quicksand? An Evaluation

of Competing Decision-making Models. *The Theory and Practice of International Relations*, ed. Fred Sondermann, William C. Olson, and David McClellan. Englewood Cliffs, NJ: Prentice-Hall.

———. *International Relations: Theories and Evidence*. Englewood Cliffs, N.J.: Prentice-Hall.

———. 1979. Foreign Policy Articulations and U.S. Conflict behavior. In *To Augur Well: Early Warning Indicators in World Politics*, ed. J. David Singer and Michael Wallace. Beverly Hills: Sage.

———. 1982. Presidential Rhetoric on Vietnam: Kennedy, Johnson, and Nixon. *International Interactions* 9 (2): 125-46.

———. 1982. Transnationalism, Power Politics, and the Realities of the Present System. In *Globalism Versus Realism: International Relations' Third Debate*, ed. Ray Maghroori and Bennett Ramberg. Boulder: Westview Press.

———. 1983. United States' National In-Security. Department of Political Science, University of Arizona, mimeo, June.

Sullivan, Michael P., and Randolph M. Siverson. 1981. Theories of War: Problems and Prospects. In *Cumulation in International Relations Research*, ed. P. Terrence Hopmann, Dina A. Zinnes, and J. David Singer. Monograph Series in World Affairs, vol. 18, bk. 3. Denver: Graduate School of International Studies.

———. 1983. The Distribution of Power and the Onset of War. *Journal of Conflict Resolution* 27 (Sept.): 473-94.

Vincent, Jack E. 1983. WEIS vs. COPDAB: Correspondence Problems. *International Studies Quarterly* 27 (June): 160-68.

Wallace, Michael D. 1973. Alliance Polarization, Cross-cutting, International War, 1815-1964. *Journal of Conflict Resolution* 17 (Dec.): 575-604.

Wanniski, Jude. 1972. A Reporter Looks Back at Vietnam. . . . *Wall Street Journal*, December 14, p. 26.

Watts, William; and Lloyd Free. 1976. A New National Survey: Nationalism, Not Isolationism. *Foreign Policy* 24 (Fall): 3-26.

Weinstein, Franklin B., and John W. Lewis. 1978. The Post-Vietnam Strategic Context in Asia. In *U.S.-Japan Relations and the Security of East Asia: The Next Decade*, ed. Franklin B. Weinstein. Boulder: Westview Press.

White, Ralph. 1951. *Value Analysis: The Nature and Use of the Method*. Society for the Psychological Study of Social Issues.

Wicker, Tom. 1968. *JFK and LBJ: The Influence of Personality upon Politics*. New York: William Morrow.

Index

Acheson, Dean, 57, 79
Afghanistan, 50, 102, 121, 164, 171–72, 179, 183
Agency for International Development, 66
Allison, Graham, 7, 8, 54, 56, 70
Angola, 121
appeasement, 134
Arizona Daily *Star*, 151, 166, 169, 174
Arizona Daily *Wildcat*, 3
Ashley, Richard, 131, 159
Asia, 15–16, 63, 91
Azar, Edward, 126

Ball, George, 63, 72, 83, 85
Berlin, 58, 65, 125
Berman, Larry, 8
Betts, Richard K., 8, 28, 56–57, 65, 67, 79, 158, 164–65
bipolarity, 125, 146, 177
Blumenthal, Sydney, 167
Bodard, Lucien, 51
Britannica Book of the Year, 18–19
Brzezinski, Zbigniew, 166
Bueno deMesquita, Bruce, 146
Bundy, McGeorge, 62
Bunker, Ellsworth, 2
bureacracy, 55, 73, 81
bureaucratic politics, 70–71, 81
Burgess, Phillip M., 126

Cambodia, 36, 39, 121, 130, 147
Canada, 16
Caribbean, 91, 173, 183

Carter, James Earl, 34, 50, 160, 162, 165, 176
Caspary, William, 119–21
Central America, 4, 16, 166, 176, 183
Central Intelligence Agency, 64
Chad, 179
Chamberlain, Neville, 134
China, 16, 131; ally of North Vietnam, 28, 48; and Communist ideology, 13, 26, 126; "loss of China," 58; rapprochement with United States, 26–27, 87, 146, 154, 175; relations with United States, 130–31, 150, 159, 180; relations with Soviet Union, 131–32, 135, 159; and Taiwan, 95
Christian Science Monitor, 26
Clifford, Clark, 75
Cold War, 152, 175; spillover from Vietnam War, 132, 154, 156; and Vietnam War, 9–10, 53, 59, 122, 124–26, 130, 134
commitment, 24–36; and behavior, 31–32, 47, 57; changes in, 33, 47, 68–69, 95; as code word, 28, 34, 79; geographic, 36; to issues, 27, 30; long-term to Vietnam, 12, 24, 28, 32, 54, 60, 80, 96; symbolic, 29–36, 39, 47, 96, 153; troop, 60–64, 74, 103, 152, 158
Communism, 180; aggression in Vietnam, 25, 48, 58, 60–61, 70, 73, 126, 153, 185–86; containment of, 8–9, 57, 59, 62, 67, 69–

Index

70, 73, 126, 150, 158, 186; perception of United States involvement, 135; as symbol, 26–27, 48; United States anticommunism, 5, 9, 12, 24–26, 59, 69, 79; victory in Vietnam, 135
Congress, United States, 103, 105–6, 121, 164, 167, 169, 175, 184
containment, 5, 8–10, 53, 62, 122, 126, 134, 150, 153
COPDAB (Conflict and Peace Data Bank), 126
Correlates of War Project, 137, 146–47
counterinsurgency, 62
Cuba, 65, 121, 166, 173; Bay of Pigs, 58, 125; missile crisis, 31, 62, 95, 125, 129, 154
Czechoslovakia, 134

DeBorchgrave, Arnaud, 164
decision-making, 11, 51–53; changes in, 49; as complex, 9; evaluation of, 76–86, 164–65; incorrect, 118, 184; incremental, 8, 24, 54–56, 65–76, 80, 82–85, 135, 153, 165; and national interest, 8; perceptions in, 12, 49; and the public, 14; rational, 8, 32, 51–54, 56–65, 70, 77, 80, 165, 185
democracy, 13, 27, 31, 34, 39
Denton, Frank, 141, 143
Department of Defense, 106
detente, 125–26, 129, 150, 154, 181–82
Diem, Ngo Dinh, 83, 185
Dien Bien Phu, 52, 95, 152
Draper, Theodore, 52, 59
Dulles, John Foster, 49, 160

Eastern Europe, 57, 125
Edelman, Murray, 25, 33
Eidenberg, Eugene, 58, 68
Eisenhower, Dwight, 12, 57, 65, 103, 125, 162–63
El Salvador, 4–5, 16, 102, 121, 166–67, 174, 176
Ellsberg, Daniel, 8, 55, 60, 71–74, 77–85
events data, 126, 133

extroversion: see moods

Ford, Gerald, 99, 163
France, 15–16, 56–57, 59–60, 66, 83, 95, 158
Free, Lloyd, 119
freedom, 13, 25–28, 34, 36, 39, 43, 48

Gallucci, Robert L., 8
Gelb, Leslie, 8, 28, 34, 54, 56–57, 59, 65–67, 73, 79, 84, 158, 164–5
Geneva Conference, 20, 95, 125
George, Alexander, 30
Geyelin, Philip, 1–2
Goldmann, Kjell, 132
Goldwater, Barry, 59, 66
Goulden, Joseph C., 70
Graff, Henry F. 27, 68
Greece, 66
Grenada, 5, 102, 173–4
Guatemala, 95, 176

Haas, Michael, 146–47
Halberstam, David, 51, 58–59, 65–66, 68, 143, 185
Hilsman, Roger, 57, 62, 67, 70, 74
Hitler, Adolph, 28, 134
Holmes, Jack, 97–99
Holsti, Kal, 29
Holsti, Ole, 117, 183
Hoopes, Townsend, 49–50, 160–62
Howell, Llewellyn, 126
human rights, 34, 50, 160, 162
Humphrey, Hubert, 9
Hungary, 28, 125
Hunter, Robert E., 123

Indochina, 57, 59, 66, 83, 85, 134–35, 158
Indonesia, 60
interventionist, 89
introversion: see moods
Iran, 4, 88, 95, 165, 171–72, 179, 183
Iraq, 88, 179
isolationism, 89–90, 119
Israel, 102, 167, 176, 179

Janis, Irving L., 8, 81

Japan, 16, 66
Johnson, Lyndon: and blame for Vietnam War, 5, 9, 52, 59, 111; commitment to Vietnam, 12, 22, 58–59, 67, 83, 158; and Congressional support, 103; doubts about the war, 45, 70, 75, 96; perceptions of options, 62, 68, 71, 83; reasons for Vietnam War, 7–8; symbolic commitment of, 8, 31–32, 37–38, 45, 49, 162; and Tonkin Gulf Resolution, 22

Kagan, Robert W., 152
Katz, Elihu, 29
Kegley, Charles, 129
Kennedy, John: and blame for Vietnam, 5, 9, 52, 74; commitment to Vietnam, 12, 57–58, 67, 72, 74, 78, 83; Congressional support for, 103; and counterinsurgency, 62; decisions about Vietnam, 20, 38, 58, 61–62, 65, 71–72, 80–81, 83–84, 158; perceptions of Vietnam, 72, 79; rhetoric, 8, 32, 37–38, 49–50, 52, 125, 160, 162
Kennedy, Robert, 70
Khrushchev, Nikita, 58, 62, 125
Kiessler, Charles A., 30
Kissinger, Henry, 27, 126
Klein, Phillip A., 88, 183
Klingberg, Frank L., 9, 89–95, 97–99, 101, 107, 118, 143, 163, 173, 180
Korean War, 79, 95, 97, 123, 125, 149, 177, 179, 182, 186

Laos, 16–17, 36, 40, 58, 65, 67, 74, 88, 130, 147
Lasswell, Harold D., 26, 34
Laurence, Edward J., 106
Lawton, Raymond W., 126
Lebanon, 4, 102, 166–67, 169, 173–74, 176, 179
Levi, Werner, 32, 123
Levy, Jack, 138–39, 141, 143, 147
Lewis, John W., 135
Libya, 179
Lindblom, Charles E., 54, 56
Lipset, Seymour Martin, 118

Lunch, William M., 111, 114, 116, 118

McCarthy, Joseph, 79
McClelland, Charles, 126
McCone, John, 64
McGovern, George, 73
McGowan, Pat, 146
McNamara, Robert, 60–61, 64, 68–69, 75, 111–12
McNaughton, James, 53, 75
Maddox, USS, 22
Mansfield, Mike, 78
Marshall Plan, 91
Mexico, 15–16
Miller, Lawrence W., 46, 96
Mitchell, Joyce M., 29
Mitchell, William C., 29
models, 6, 25, 76–77
Modelski, George, 145, 148
moods, 9, 87–90, 93–95, 97, 102, 108, 118–19, 121, 180–81
Moorsteen, Richard, 82
Morse, Edward L., 123
Moss, Robert, 164
Moyers, Bill, 68
Mueller, John E., 103, 114

Nacht, Michael, 5, 62
Nardin, Terry, 164
national interest, 8, 24–25, 34, 114
National Security Council, 57, 67, 70
Newmark, Todd L., 152
New York Times, 31, 69, 75, 152, 158
Nicaragua, 166, 176
Nixon, Richard: blame for Vietnam, 5; commitment to Vietnam, 12; Congressional support for, 103; and detente, 126, 130, 146, 154, 175, 181; perceptions of Vietnam, 8–9; public opinion of, 116; rhetoric of, 26, 32, 39, 99, 102, 161; settlement of war, 73; widening of war, 130
North Atlantic Treaty Organization, 125, 132
North Korea, 27–28, 158
North Vietnam, 36, 48–49, 59, 61,

Index

63, 68, 74, 96, 103, 121, 129, 134, 165

O'Donnell, Kenneth, 78
Organization of Petroleum Exporting Countries, 175

Papers of the President, 15, 34, 37, 161
Paraguay, 15
Partial Test Ban Treaty, 130
Pearl Harbor, 90–91, 95, 183
Pentagon Papers: attention to Vietnam, 20–21, 77–78; decisions on Vietnam, 70–71, 74, 80–81; and early aid to Vietnam, 56, 61, 65, 158; and justification of Vietnam War, 20–21, 58, 63, 68; and Robert McNamara, 111; and Tonkin Gulf, 22
Peoples Republic of China: see China
Pfeiffer, Richard M., 51
Philippines, 36, 91
Phillips, Warren, 141, 143
Pleiku, 67–68
Point Four, 91
Poland, 50, 102
Pool, Ithiel deSola, 31, 34
public opinion, 9, 87, 97, 103, 107–9, 112–19, 153, 173–74, 186
Pueblo, USS, 27

Rapaport, Anatol, 98
Ravenal, Earl C., 3
Reagan, Ronald, 4, 99, 101–2, 114, 121, 152, 162, 166–67, 169, 173, 176, 184
Reston, James, 58
rhetoric, 3, 8, 25–28, 37, 45, 47. *See also* symbols
Roberts, Chalmers M., 52
Rolling Thunder, 68
Rood, Robert M., 146
Rosenau, James, 29, 117, 183
Roskin, Michael, 90, 103
Rostow, Walt, 20, 38, 60
Rusk, Dean, 27, 61
Russett, Bruce, 169, 171–72

Saigon, 1–2, 60, 96, 121, 135, 158
Sandinistas, 166
Schell, Jonathan, 52–53
Schlesinger, Arthur, 52, 55, 71, 80
Schoenbrun, David, 59
Schwarz, John, 152
Scott, Peter Dale, 51
Senate, United States, 106–7
Sheehan, Neil, 30, 56, 60–64, 67–69, 80, 158
Sigelman, Lee, 46, 96
Simon, Herbert, 55
Singer, J. David, 137, 139–141, 143, 146, 177
Siverson, Randolph, 123, 136
Slater, Jerome, 164
Small, Melvin, 137, 139–141, 143, 146, 177
Somoza, Anastasio, 166
Sorenson, Ted, 52
Southeast Asia, 3, 57–58, 60–62, 65, 122, 155, 186
South Korea, 16–17, 28, 66, 95
South Vietnam, 1, 13, 36, 61–63, 67–70, 73–74, 80, 83
Soviet Union, 26, 149, 177; aid to Central America, 166; ally of Cuba, 121; and Cold War, 10; and detente, 146, 150; and Eastern Europe, 125; ideology of, 13; invasion of Afghanistan, 50, 102, 164, 179, 183; invasion of Czechoslovakia, 134; invasion of Hungary, 28, 125; power of, 175; relations with China, 131, 159; relations with United States, 50, 57–58, 95, 121, 126, 129–32, 134–35, 150, 154, 159, 173, 180–81; shooting down of U–2, 125, 182; target of U.S. communication, 48
Spanish-American War, 94
Sperlich, Peter, 111–14, 116, 118
Spitzer, Robert J., 105
State of the Union Address, 93–94, 99–102, 105, 107, 119, 121, 154, 162, 173
Sullivan, Michael P., 8, 31–32, 38, 43, 45, 123, 136, 139, 144, 175
symbols, 25–39, 45, 47, 99, 153, 160

Taiwan, 95
Taylor, Maxwell, 20, 38, 60–62, 67, 80, 84
Tet, 27, 69, 75
Thailand, 36, 74
Tonkin Gulf, 20–23, 59, 70, 130
Truman, Harry, 12, 56, 73, 158
Turkey, 16–17, 66
Turner Joy, USS, 22

United Kingdom, 16–17, 57, 66

Vance, Cyrus, 165–67, 169
Vienna Summit, 58
Vietcong, 26, 62, 68, 74, 75
Vietminh, 57, 158
Vietnam. *See* North Vietnam; South Vietnam
Vietnamization, 97
Vietnam War: attention to, 7–8, 14–17, 20, 24, 35; escalation of, 43, 75, 108, 112–13, 130; justifications of, 20–24, 99; perceptions of, 8, 40–43

Vincent, Jack, 126

Wallace, Michael, 146
Wanniski, Jude, 185
war, definitions of, 138–39
War of 1812, 94
War of League of Venice, 138
War Powers Act, 169
Warsaw Treaty Organization, 132
Watts, William, 119
Weinstein, Franklin B., 135
Westmoreland, William, 75
White, Ralph, 34
Wicker, Tom, 58–59, 65–67
Wittkopf, Eugene, 129
World War I, 27, 31, 94, 143, 177, 179
World War II, 12–13, 27, 31, 94–95, 97, 122–23, 125, 143, 177, 179, 182

Zaire, 4–5, 121, 165

www.ingramcontent.com/pod-product-compliance
Lightning Source LLC
Chambersburg PA
CBHW032043150426
43194CB00006B/408